everyday radiance

365 ZODIAC-INSPIRED PROMPTS
for SELF-CARE & SELF-RENEWAL

HEIDI ROSE ROBBINS

Illustrated by DANIEL BARRETO

CHRONICLE BOOKS
SAN FRANCISCO

Introduction

I had an unusual childhood.

My dad was an astrologer in Fargo, North Dakota, and he may have been the only one. I grew up watching him draw up charts at the kitchen table and read astrology books at all hours of the morning and night. He even opened a metaphysical bookstore one block from our house. It was called The Question Shoppe.

So it's probably not surprising that at the age of three, I learned the zodiac along with the alphabet. As a teenager, I never had a friend come to the house without my father asking her birthday and offering some thoughts about her strengths and inherent gifts. By the time I turned nineteen, my dad was holding conferences about soul-centered astrology and I was becoming more curious about his profession. I wanted to see for myself what this was all about. And once I started studying astrology, there was no turning back.

Astrology means "the study of the stars." And we've been doing that for thousands of years. We have looked to the heavens to know when to plant and harvest, move, go to war, or marry. We have been touched by the beauty of Venus resting low in the sky. We have celebrated solstices and equinoxes, celestial events deeply connected to our relationship with the heavenly bodies. Our very language holds the love affair humanity has enjoyed with the heavens since the beginning. The word "consider," for example, comes from Latin roots, *con* and *sider*, which together mean "with the stars."

Today, we can use astrology in infinitely practical and profoundly inspiring ways. It can offer clarity, instruction, and encouragement about our life's journey. It can remind us that we are part of an intricate tapestry, and the cycles of our lives mirror greater cycles at work. We are here to play a part in a symphony being composed over and throughout time. What is our note to sound? What is our greatest offering? What can we give that is ours, most uniquely, to give? Astrology is an exquisite tool that can offer perspective and guidance.

Everyday Radiance provides an opportunity to engage with the astrological energies that are available each month. The book is divided into the twelve months of the astrological year, and each month offers insight into a different zodiacal sign. There are prompts and practices, writing exercises and meditations. I hope that you will engage with this book in joyful and practical ways and use it to learn more about your most radiant self.

Keep it by your bed and read it first thing or carry it in your bag for lunchtime inspiration. I invite you to engage with it on a daily basis. May each day's offering remind you of the beauty and brilliance that you are!

Big love,
HEIDI ROSE

Some Basic Astrology for Our Journey Together

When I first started practicing astrology, I mostly did charts for artists and seekers. Now, I do charts daily for stockbrokers, lawyers, CEOs, and scientists. Astrology is rapidly becoming a more accepted and accessible language. Though not everyone wants to study astrology, most are interested in what it can teach us about ourselves and the unfolding of our lives.

This book is not meant to be a complete introduction to astrology, but to get the most out of it, it may be beneficial to understand a few of the basics. To that end, let's explore a few key qualities for each sign as well as the sun, the moon, and the rising sign—the three big positions of our astrological chart.

Here are a few key qualities of each sign:

ARIES MARCH 20–APRIL 19
bold, pioneering, impulsive, bright

TAURUS APRIL 20–MAY 20
steady, intuitive, transparent

GEMINI MAY 21–JUNE 20
communicative, unifying, fact-finding, curious

CANCER JUNE 21–JULY 21
nourishing, compassionate, resourceful, sensitive

LEO JULY 22–AUGUST 22
expressive, sovereign, generous, authentic

VIRGO AUGUST 23–SEPTEMBER 21
devoted, hard-working, health-conscious, discerning

LIBRA SEPTEMBER 22–OCTOBER 22
peace-making, diplomatic, fair

SCORPIO OCTOBER 23–NOVEMBER 21
deep, intimate, strategic, powerful

SAGITTARIUS NOVEMBER 22–DECEMBER 20
visionary, focused, goal-oriented, athletic

CAPRICORN DECEMBER 21–JANUARY 19
disciplined, committed, authoritative

AQUARIUS JANUARY 20–FEBRUARY 17
innovative, cooperative, objective

PISCES FEBRUARY 18–MARCH 19
imaginative, redemptive, loving, artistic

These key words will help you home in on the essential themes of each month so you can engage with the energies with greater clarity and commitment.

The Sun, Moon, and Rising Signs

When it comes to the three key positions in the astrological chart, most of us know our sun sign. If I asked you, "What's your sign?" most people would respond by saying, "I'm a Taurus." Or "I'm a Gemini." The sun spends four weeks in each sign of the zodiac. We are all born on a certain day in a certain month and this is what determines our sun sign. The sun sign reveals a lot about our day-to-day work or our everyday personality. We all want to use the best qualities of our sun sign.

The moon position (represented by a crescent moon in the chart) reflects our childhood. The sign in which the moon falls is where we feel very comfortable, safe, or familiar. There are also habitual behaviors associated with the moon sign that we need to outgrow or evolve. If you know the position of your moon, you might want to focus on that particular sign to study the best ways to both outgrow habitual behaviors that no longer serve you and invite more conscious and productive ways of using the energy. If, for example, you are an Aries Moon, the entries and prompts between March 20th and April 19th (approximately) will give you ideas about how to grow and evolve the qualities of Aries in your life.

The rising sign is determined by your exact time of birth (the sign that was rising over the eastern horizon the moment you were born), and it represents our highest calling. This is the sign to which we can apprentice. It invites us to offer the best of the sign as a gift to others. Again, if you know your rising sign, you can spend extra time focused on that month of the year. If I am Capricorn rising, I want to do anything and everything to grow the most positive qualities of Capricorn and offer them as my gift in the world, so, in this book, I'd be sure to explore all the days between approximately December 21st and January 19th to learn about those positive qualities.

When we know these three key positions, we know the energies available to us from our past, our present and our ever-unfolding future. We have an astrological assignment given through our sun, moon, and rising signs. In the upcoming section "How to Use this Book," you will be given an opportunity to look up your astrological chart and learn your unique sun, moon, and rising sign.

How to Use This Book

Everyday Radiance is a book of astrological encouragement! Whether you were born during the month of Aries, Taurus, Aquarius, or Pisces, this book offers you a chance to embody and understand the signs you pass through during a typical year, and harness their energy for yourself more fully. I will offer many different ways of exploring each sign throughout the month and I will invite you to engage with it through writing, movement, and reflection.

The astrological New Year begins with the first sign of the zodiac, the sign of Aries. We will do the same! The book begins as we welcome the first and most fiery sign. We'll wrap up the year with Pisces, the last sign of the zodiac. But feel free to open and start this book on any day—its content is evergreen and not specific to any year.

In addition to an open mind and heart, there are a few optional but helpful things that will make this journey together exceptional:

1. A journal. I ask questions and offer writing prompts and creativity nudges for each sign, and it would be helpful for you to have a dedicated place to explore these. It doesn't have to be a beautiful journal. It can be an inexpensive spiral notebook. You just need some blank pages and a pen you love.

2. A friend. Find a friend and engage in the full year together. It can be fun and rewarding to read each other your writing prompts and be accountable to each other. Your friendship will be stronger and deeper having gone on this journey together.

3. A willingness to dive deeper. Sometimes, I'll suggest that you read certain poems or pieces of writing to complement certain days. Some of the poems I wrote myself. *All* of these poems are quickly and easily found at www.heidirose.com/poetry. Take the time to look them up. And please do take the time to read them slowly and out loud. Reading poetry aloud changes the texture of the words and your understanding of them.

4. Know your sun, moon, and rising sign. Many astrological sites can generate your chart for free, but you can also order your chart at www.heidirose.com. You'll receive your beautiful unique astrological chart with a list of all your planetary positions—including the sun, moon and rising sign. Again, this is not necessary to use this book, but adds subtlety and deeper insight to your experience.

I'm so glad you're here to take this journey with a community of fellow explorers. May your daily engagement with this book inspire you to be more fully encouraged and radiant in your days.

Aries

Welcoming Aries

Aries launches the astrological New Year! It offers the gift of a fresh start. After the fire, after the loss, after the dying, after the culmination, the graduation, the end, the winter, Aries enters and offers the vitality of spring—the bravado of youth. Aries says, "Do not despair. It takes just a single step to move in a new direction." Even if we are tired, sad, reluctant, or afraid, Aries can help us take that single step. What wants to begin today in each of us? What requires our daring? What quality do we wish to move toward or cultivate? Aries offers fuel for our future. It offers the seed for our blossoming, the first necessary yes for our next great initiative. Today, we can choose willingness. We can take tiny steps in the direction of whatever it is we wish to grow. Today is ours to begin. Let's meet it and open to all it offers.

INVITATION

Today, I want to ask: What is in bud in you? What still wants to blossom? What is ripe to unfold, unfurl, open? What quality is present in you but wants to strengthen?

Go Last

Let's practice going last. Aries likes to be first, loves the front of the line, and often takes off before anyone else has even started. So on an Aries day, when we all feel a little fiery and feisty, let's call in patience. Let's trust that everything is unfolding in good time and we need not rush. The philosopher and spiritual teacher Jiddu Krishnamurti always insisted on being the last person in the buffet line during meals at his school. It was a gesture of humility and generosity. He was patient and at ease, enjoying his time in line instead of waiting for the moment when it would be his turn. The fire of Aries sometimes prevents us from being fully in the beauty of now. So today let us eagerly raise our hands and say, "I'm happy to go last!"

INVITATION

When it comes to waiting for the bus or ordering coffee, notice how you feel in line and experiment with letting others go before you. Practice appreciating the moment you're in—the sights and sounds—rather than hoping it passes quickly. Practice trusting that you are not behind but, instead, exactly where you need to be.

The Power to Originate

Aries isn't always about action. At its best, the energy of Aries can be about receiving and saying yes to a soul message or idea—the power to originate. We've all had a moment when we've been given something, when we've received an idea that is ours to grow. It's a thrilling moment. It's a quiet, potent moment. It's a moment when we know we have to be initiators in our own lives. We know we must summon the dynamic energy and assertiveness of Aries to see this idea through.

INVITATION

What idea is yours to cultivate? Feel and know yourself to be the daring leader of your own life. Today, practice saying yes to the new idea and taking a first action step. Take a cleansing breath. Go forth.

Quiet Beginnings

It's easy to think that every beginning must be bold. Perhaps today we can remind ourselves that when we plant a seed, it takes time for the seed to sprout. Much of the early growth is invisible— it is being quietly nourished in rich soil. Aries loves to see big and immediate results, but some of the most powerful beginnings happen with a quiet discovery or an inner affirmation or a single step in a new direction. Let's ask ourselves, what have we quietly begun recently? Are we feeling impatient for results? What if we just keep watering the seed daily with a ton of trust? What if we think to ourselves, *I've begun; it's underway.* What if we all took a little step back to remember that so often we don't allow ourselves to enjoy the beginnings of things because we're already imagining vibrant fruition. Beginnings are beautiful, like babies are beautiful. We can look at them and smile and appreciate them in all forms. Today, let's celebrate tiny steps and loving launches and patience. There's time, plenty of time, for everything to unfold.

INVITATION

Buy a tiny plant. Or plant a seed. Water it. Care for it. Watch it grow. Nourish it as you nourish your new idea. The act of watering a plant daily nourishes both the plant and the self.

The Power of One

Here is a very Aries poem I wrote, "One." Read this poem slowly and out loud:

One (intimate) glance
can open something
long closed
within us.

One (full) breath
can ease
an ancient fear.

One (tender) touch
can soothe
unspeakable pain.

One (loving) word
can soften
the armored heart.

One (radical) thought
can spark
unfathomable daring.

One (courageous) step
can change forever
the course of a life.

INVITATION

Choose one of the stanzas and let it work on you. Which stanza would you like to bring to life? Dare yourself to take ONE step today.

Aries

Dawn

Each dawn carries the Aries energy. Aries is the first light, renewal, the chance to begin again. No matter how dark the night has been, Aries, like the dawn, initiates light. Aries reminds us that the first light inspires greater light. Aries says, "Assert your soul self." It invites us to step forward or offer what we've got into the world and to let the light grow. Mars and Mercury are the planets most connected to Aries. We invite the daring strength of Mars and the intelligence and innovation of Mercury into our day and we let them dance. We remember every bold beginning moves us somewhere new. Today, let the spirit of dawn rise in you. Let the sun ignite your heart and step out into the new day.

INVITATION

Sometime this week, set your alarm to watch the sun rise, even if you just open your curtains, climb back in bed, and watch the light return. As the sun returns, feel the light rise in you.

Daring

Daring often involves action over time. It might be about showing up in a new way for ourselves day after day or practicing a new way of being. Daring might be about ending an old cycle that no longer serves who we are becoming. Daring might be a powerful yes or a potent no. Daring is always about breathing life into our passion and purpose. How might we be more daring in our lives starting now? Where do we feel daring in our bodies? What truly is the next most daring action we could take in our lives? What is standing in our way? Is there a way we might clear the obstruction and take the leap?

INVITATION

Assign yourself a dare. Is there some action you can take on the dare today? Tell a friend about your dare so you are more likely to follow through! (And yes, it can be a *small* dare.)

Aries

Red

Aries is carmine red. Scarlet red. The children's game Red Rover, Red Rover. Red lips. Red car, red blood, red rage, red meat. Ruby red, red apple, red flame, red wine. Red pine, cherry red, red hot (Again! Again!), Red hot! Red alert, red fox. Code red, Little Red Riding Hood (Was she an Aries?). Red letter day. Can you feel the vitality and potency and a few cautionary words about Aries? Now go forth and try not to run any red lights!

INVITATION

Red ignites courage. Wear something red today. See how it makes you feel. Let the red of Aries inspire you to be bold.

Refuse the Old Song

It's easy to fall into a mental loop of all that is broken or wretched. Today, let's refuse the same old song. There are birds singing outside our windows. We are alive and possibility is always present. No matter how weary, we can summon our inner nine-year-old and remember how glorious it was to wake up on a spring day and feel the delight of the hours before us. I'm sure many of us are working all day today, but that doesn't mean we can't feel a shred of delight. Aries reminds us we have access to renewal at any hour. Even right now, let's befriend any grumpiness, frustration, or sadness, but not let it hold us back from the discovery of something beautiful or vitalizing today. What new song can we begin to sing?

INVITATION

A good soundtrack clears the way for a new attitude. Listen to something that jostles you out of a habitual loop today and sing along. When we sing, we can't help but express the truth of the moment and release what needs releasing to make room for the new.

Aries

Our Aries Friends

Here are the reasons it's great to have an Aries friend:

1. They are forerunners and always invite you to join them in the new.

2. They are daring and willing to step forward when others are not.

3. They have original new ideas that spark us into action.

4. They are gloriously and sometimes not so gloriously impatient, and they get us all moving.

5. They are feisty and fiery and bold.

6. They will encourage you to hurry up and do the thing you said you were going to do.

7. They love to create new things.

8. They embody youthfulness, which can help keep us all feeling a little spry.

9. They carry the energy of spring and with it, the energy of possibility.

10. They love initiating, setting off, beginnings, and fresh starts.

Celebrate your Aries pal today!

INVITATION

Let's reach out to one (or more!) of our Aries pals and thank them for their friendship. We might even send them a list of why we love them!

Everything Is Not at Stake

Aries has a sense of urgency. It exists in fight or flight. That is, we live as if everything is at stake, every moment. We live as if we're waiting for the starting gun to fire for the Olympic 100-yard dash. Adrenaline pumps. This is particularly so for those of us with lots of Aries, Leo, or Sagittarius already in our charts. Let's use this Aries energy to break through. Let's dare ourselves to face our inner dragons or dare ourselves to speak. We can dare ourselves to believe in all we have to offer or dare ourselves to be leaders. But we can also dare ourselves to stop and breathe and say gently to ourselves, "In this moment, everything is not at stake. There's no need to rush or panic. All will unfold in perfect timing. In this moment, the only necessity is to breathe, quiet down, and trust."

INVITATION

Say this out loud: "Everything is not at stake." Accompany these words with three deep breaths. Return to this phrase though out the day.

Aries

Yell

Sometimes we have to yell. And by that, I mean, let strong, directed, conscious energy move through our throat center at a high volume. Why? Because sometimes we all need to wake up, be startled out of our own lethargy or habitual behavior. Think of it as a howl of love, a yell because we all know better. It clears the way for more light. It cleans out the gunk. We don't have to attack. We can sound an awakening cry. It calls us to attention and demands that we listen.

INVITATION

Yell today, whether it's into your pillow or somewhere out in nature. Give yourself permission to make a lot of noise. Allow your own private yell to wake you up.

Kazam

There's a physicality, energy, and momentum to the three fire signs: Aries, Leo, and Sagittarius. Cartoon sound effects come to mind: *Bang! Oof! Kazam! Pow! Crash!* There's excitement and vitality. We are on the move. Everything speeds up. Let's try to enjoy the buzz, the new ideas, the sense of possibility. If we channel this vital energy for the good we can take clear, simple action. Go ahead and move forward if you feel delighted, inspired, and ready. If not, just use this fiery energy to feel vital and alive. Let this day feel lighter, more playful, improvised, and enlivened.

INVITATION

Use this fiery energy to make up a few cartoon exclamations today, and find any excuse to greet someone with them. Commit entirely— we don't play enough! Play brings delight, and delight makes way for authentic self-expression.

Aries

Calm

Aries is known for impulsivity, running headlong into the next chapter, accelerating quickly and diving in. It's also frequently noted for its impatience. Aries feels everyone is moving too slowly. However, the key to growing and evolving any sign is to bring a greater consciousness to the tricky bits. With Aries, the key is to begin, yes, but to begin with patience, to begin calmly. Whenever we are working to express a greater wisdom through any sign, we have to welcome its opposite. Aries welcomes Libra, and learns to pause and weigh decisions before leaping. It learns diplomacy and consideration of others. It learns to lean in the direction of harmony and poise instead of the fight. Of course, there are perfect moments to cut loose and let Aries do its thing. It's smart, quick, bold, and goes for it. And there's nothing like a leap. But maybe today we can all have a day of new cool ideas, calmly initiated.

INVITATION

Think of one area of your life where you'd benefit from an immediate leap, and another where it would be good to assess and pause. Explore both through reflection or journaling.

Solitude

An Aries day is a perfect day to fly solo. Time alone can be delicious; we get to move at our unique pace, and the needs of the rest of the world fall away. We can let ourselves be as fiery and feisty as we need to be without butting anyone else with our big Aries ram horns. Even if we don't need solo time on an Aries day, it's always good to take the time to breathe and listen within. That's often when the great ideas come knocking. There is nothing sad about solitude. It is deeply nourishing when we treat ourselves as our own best company.

INVITATION

Make a conscious choice today to do one thing solo: lunch, a walk in the park, write, read a good book at a coffee shop. Notice how it feels to be with your solo self—is there anxiety, pure bliss, or uncertainty? Focus on staying connected to your solo self today.

Aries

Bright Ideas

Mars rules Aries at the personality level and Mercury rules Aries at the soul level. When Mars and Mercury work together most effectively, they can manifest powerful ideas in us. Mercury says, "I have something new to say," and Mars says, "Nothing is stopping you from stepping forth to say it!" As Mercury works though Aries, it unearths great ideas. Then it calls on the entrepreneurial spirit, dynamic energy, and assertiveness of Mars to dive in and act. Aries asks us to be the daring leader of our own life. It helps us all overcome procrastination, fear, or hopelessness. Its rallying cry is always, "What are we waiting for?"

INVITATION

Grab a crisp blank sheet of paper and some markers. Give yourself 15 to 20 minutes to write all the great ideas you've had recently. Don't edit yourself—just write all the things that you might just want to try or do. Keep writing. It doesn't have to be a list. You can write all over the page! When you are done, put it away for a bit and then return to it in a week or two and see what stands out.

Conditions Are Never Perfect

Let's ask ourselves: What is the first step we can take today? In other words, how can we use the initiating energy of Aries to move forward in a way that supports us? What is one tiny action that would feel good to take? We can ask ourselves, "What's something we've been talking about doing, but haven't quite been doing?" Aries is a kind of now-or-never, do-or-die sign. The best of that energy is offered through the spark of first action. Let's not wait for the conditions to be perfect. Let's catch our own selves off guard and find ourselves launching before we can come up with an excuse not to.

INVITATION

Ask yourself, "What is the next right step for me today?" This can get the ball rolling. Maybe you've been talking a lot about writing: Set the timer and write for 15 minutes. Maybe you've been promising yourself you'd move a bit more: The minute you finish reading this, walk around the block. Practice a quick inner *Yes* to the first step before you talk yourself out of it!

Aries

Patience

Here's an important Aries question: How can we be more patient with ourselves and everyone else? This is not so easy for an Aries. The Aries rallying cry is "Hurry up! Buck up! Get on with it already, or I'll just plunge in and make it happen." We can always use Aries to launch or dare, but we can also use Aries time to practice impulse control. If we could all practice waiting a few minutes before leaping, yelling, or tweeting, our world might begin to feel very different.

INVITATION

How quickly do you turn your impatience inward? Do you berate yourself for not making everything happen faster? Notice how impatience dances in your life with these two writing prompts: "Hurry up!" and "I have all the time I need to. . . ."

Firsts

Aries rules all firsts. Let's remember some firsts: your first kiss, your first friend, the first time you drove a car. Remember your first taste of freedom. Remember your first big trip, your first sip of coffee, the first time you got really sick. Remember the first teacher you really loved or the first time you failed a test. Remember meeting someone you knew would be in your life forever. It was new. How did you feel?

INVITATION

Write about any first in your life.

APRIL 7

It Is I Who Must Begin

Vaclav Havel wrote a poem entitled "It Is I Who Must Begin." The first line of the poem is the title. Let's take a minute right now and speak those words out loud. These are words whispered to our heart and a gift to focus our mind. They offer strength. We can say yes at any moment we choose. We must decide to offer ourselves to journey forth, to take the first step. Aries is the springtime to our dark winter hour. It is the spark of possibility, amid futility or hopelessness. It is the forerunner in undiscovered terrain. When we each dare to begin, the power of our collective courageous selves blazes forth.

INVITATION

Let the power of Havel's words live in you throughout the day. Let them inform your choices. If you are feeling nervous about speaking up, just whisper them to yourself. Let the words fuel you!

Just Do It

Is there anything on our life-work-home checklist that we can just do? We all sometimes have action items on our to-do list for weeks, months, and, dare I say, years. Aries responds to that with "Why are you making it so complicated? Let's just make the call, change the light bulb, write the newsletter, take a walk." Aries is impatient in a delicious way. It stamps its foot and says "Enough! Let's just do this thing!"

INVITATION

Compile an action list. Record one action item that will feel great, affirming, relieving, or exciting to act on today. Aries says, "If not me, then who? If not now, then when?" What tiny action items or bold moves does today hold for you? Check in with a pal and see if anyone needs an extra nudge to do the same.

Aries

Walk Lightly

It's going to be OK. Everything that feels broken or raw or not enough, let it be. Rock it to sleep. Smooth your brow. Everything is in the process of unfolding, evolving, mending. Nothing stays broken forever. Every ache, every sadness will find its way to healing, to softening. Let be. Let yourself be. Nothing is forever. We are all in bud. We are all finding our way to be touched by the sun. We're all slowly daring to open. We are all brave and scared, broken and whole, tired and renewed, hopeless and full of prom-ise. Quiet now, loves. Start your day gently. Stay as soft and open as you are in sleep. Do not pick up your burdens yet. Walk lightly into this new day. It is already whispering its gifts. Put your hand on your heart and breathe.

INVITATION

Find kind words for yourself this morning. Take three deep breaths and go back and read the message above to yourself. Whisper it and read it slowly. Receive it as you read it.

Love Like a Wild Thing

Breathe in fiery initiative. Breathe in springtime love. Breathe in the fire of purification, the ability to renew, reset, begin again. Aries is quick to act and loves to light little fires. Let's use that energy to send little fiery love messages. Tell someone why you love them. Tell them one reason they inspire you. Offer them sweet kindling to keep their hearth, heart, home alight. We need messages of hope and love. Aries says, "Say it! Say it now, say it loud and clear. Dare to love like a wild thing." Let's grow the light we all need with our messages of love.

INVITATION

Write a little love message—email, text, or a real letter—sometime today. You could leave it under a magnet on the refrigerator. You could mail it across the globe. You could leave it for a stranger at the coffee shop. It could be anonymous or deeply personal.

You Are Perfectly on Time

Remember the rabbit in *Alice's Adventures in Wonderland*? He's late, he's late, for a very important date. In Aries we always feel like we're not going fast enough. We're three steps ahead, sure that we are three steps behind, lunging toward the next thing. We don't have time. In Aries, we can enjoy the fire, the zing, and the leap, but we might also pause a moment now and then and arrive fully in the present. Mars-driven Aries needs a little Venus. Venus reminds us that sometimes it's more powerful to attract what we need instead of hurling ourselves forward to grasp it. You're not late, Aries. You're perfectly on time. Take a breath and relax. You'll be on your feisty, fiery way soon enough.

INVITATION

Try simply using the phrase "I am perfectly on time" throughout your day. Use it when working at home. Use it on the way to meet a friend. Use it when you start to think that you are behind in the manifesting of life's big dreams. "I am perfectly on time."

Morning Light

Here is a poem, "Morning Light," I wrote one early morning in Ojai, California. Read it slowly and out loud:

The early hour.
The scent of something past.
The growing light in the sky.
The wisp of cloud.
The crispness of morning.
The chisel of the mountaintop.
The rawness of my heart.
The whisper of the possible.
The ripening of the orange grove.
The stillness that softens.
The bowl of tea.
The new face in the mirror.

INVITATION

When you next look in the mirror, see if you can say hello to someone new. See if you can surprise yourself with something in yourself that you haven't noticed before. What quality is emerging as you gaze at yourself anew?

Freely Forward

Let's shake a little springtime vitality into our beings. Let's refuse the known route. Let's not hold back. Let's be bold with what we want to say and summon the power to begin again that Aries so generously pours forth. Let's not wait to be inspired—let's inspire ourselves. Have you ever been stuck in a traffic jam for too long and then finally everything begins to flow? Let's release ourselves to drive freely forward. What is it you wish to begin? How do you wish to be bold? What project in your life requires a dose of the vitality of spring?

INVITATION

Work to physically embody and feel this vital energy today. Find a good solid surface, like a wall, to push up against. Now, lean into the wall and push with all your might. Push for thirty seconds if you can. And then release. Feel all the tingly, light energy pouring through you. Feel released to move forward.

The Wisdom of Saturn

The youth of Aries sometimes requires the wisdom of Saturn. The desire to act, move forward, bust through, get on with it, is strong, but tempered by Saturn, these ideas might actually take root and grow. So today let's listen to our wise selves, slow down, and feel our own authority. Excitement will want to win the day, but let wisdom speak as well. Don't let Saturn crush or subdue the dream. Instead let's use Saturn to begin wisely, launch with clarity, invite patience to play with passion. We can pace ourselves for a marathon, not a sprint. Welcome fire, but carefully tend the flame. Feed it with moderation and clarity. Say, "Yes, yes, all in good time and with a plan!"

INVITATION

Think of a wise person in your life. How do you feel when in their presence? We often inherently slow down and arrive more fully in the potent present moment when we are in the presence of wisdom. Cultivate this feeling even when alone. Act from this place.

Aries

Goodwill across the Globe

Aries rules the power of a good idea. Here are a few:

1. Let silence nourish you today.

2. Envision humanity working cooperatively to heal.

3. Slow down, even more.

4. Connect with your soul self and listen, then write what you hear.

5. Say a loving prayer for humanity.

6. Imagine lines of light emerging from the fire of your heart, connecting with other people of goodwill across the globe.

7. Imagine the planet Earth encircled with light.

8. Let someone know you love them. And that includes yourself. You can also send your "I love you" through time and space.

9. Walk gently.

10. Breathe deeply.

INVITATION

Choose one or two of these suggestions today. Share with a friend! Review at the end of your day. Were you able to integrate one or two? How did it feel?

Sometimes It's Hazy

Hazy times are thresholds for the gentle entrance of the unknown. When we no longer know ourselves inside out, we are softening into necessary change. Our edges get blurry; and blurry can lead to new beginnings. Tender and tentative can lead to clarity and truth. Bewildered will unfold into beautiful and bold. Just give it time. Let's trust what feels wobbly and confusing. Let's trust the circuitous path. Life is not linear. It is a sacred labyrinth of twists and turns, loss and rebirth, meditations and manifestations. Let's trust the in-betweens, the not quite yet, and the who am I now?

INVITATION

Put your hands on your heart and take a few breaths. Whisper: "I don't know yet. I don't know yet, and that's OK."

Aries

Arise

As we approach the month of Taurus, let's remind ourselves of the true Aries calling. If we play with the letters in Aries, we easily come upon *arise*—which is a stirring word. There is something so strong and commanding and hopeful in it. Let's say it out loud: Arise! It beckons us to lift, come forth, elevate. Aries loves to arise, improve, engage with, and enjoy the world.

INVITATION

Let's write. Put the word *arise* at the top of the page. What does it stir in you? What do you want to say? Why should you arise?

Ripe with Possibility

Aries is like a sunrise, a door opening, and a ride in a fast car all rolled into one. It's the action of "ready, set, go!" We feel stronger, bolder, and braver under Aries and more willing to just do it. We feel ready to celebrate the new, and what is in bud in each of our lives. Let's ask ourselves: What do we feel pressing to the surface that wants bright, colorful expression? What quality wants to come to the fore and present itself? This last day of Aries is ripe with possibility. Let's contemplate what quality or qualities we want to unfurl in our lives with the help of this last day of the Aries season—this time of bright beginnings.

INVITATION

Write a few qualities you'd like to unfurl in your life or that you'd like to see grow through Taurus season. Share them with a friend.

Aries

Taurus

Welcoming Taurus

Today, we welcome Taurus, the great sign of illumination and manifestation. With Venus as one of its primary rulers, Taurus is a sign that manifests the beautiful and grows the light. It rules fertility, fecundity, and blossoming. The flowers of our lives start to grow. Seeds planted under Aries break soil and that which we value and wish to nourish begins to fill the garden of our lives. Taurus reminds us that no garden can be rushed into its fullness. The month of Taurus slows us down in the best of ways. So many of us move so fast and have so much on our plate that we forget all the beauty—nature and nourishment, family and romance. Taurus reminds us to fully appreciate our lives. It is ever willing to rhythmically, steadily, and humbly do good work and attend to what is valuable. Let's welcome Taurus and all its beauty, magnetism, and potency.

INVITATION

Let's begin the Taurus season with a simple walk somewhere lovely. Stop for a moment and take a few deep breaths in front of anything you find beautiful. If we intentionally soften the whole front surface of our body—our face, our chest, our belly—we render ourselves more available for the beauty that wants to enter. You can walk slowly and receive.

Patience

Taurus welcomes rhythms that soothe us. It appreciates the natural and cyclic unfolding of the seasons, the beating of our heart, and the simple beauty of the inhale and exhale. Taurus falls in the thick of spring in the Northern Hemisphere and welcomes the mystery of what is happening beneath the soil, just beneath the surface. It celebrates the pulse underground and celebrates the seed that is racking open and making its way toward the light. We can feel the green pushing fiercely and fully through the soil. We can feel both the urgency and the patience of sprouting life. We can listen for the beauty as it makes its way through the quiet earth and trust its timing. Patience makes way for wild blossoming.

INVITATION

Watch time-lapse photography of a seed sprouting. Feel that same process happening with something that is growing in your life. Or actually plant seeds in a patch of earth and tend to them. See if you can catch the moment the soil breaks to new life and presents its beauty.

Beauty

In chaotic times, we need the rich beauty of Taurus more than ever. Beauty replenishes and revives. It calms the nervous system. Beauty redeems. Every day is a day to name and celebrate the beautiful. Let's acknowledge the tiny buds of our lives and the fuller blossoming. And let's remember beauty can make its presence known even in our most broken spaces within and without. There is always a purple crocus bursting through a sea of concrete. When we name the beauty we see, we help it grow. Let's breathe and look out our window and let our eyes land on one beautiful thing and let's praise it, talk to it. "You lovely thing. Almost budding pink, pink rose. Thank you. Keep lavishly unfolding. I see you."

INVITATION

Let's see if we can use every sense today to name the beautiful. What beauty will you taste? What beauty will you smell? Touch? See? Hear? Name it and thank it. Feel how beauty actually shifts something inside us when we acknowledge and receive it.

Solidity

Taurus is solid. There is something so good, true, reliable, and calming about Taurus. It is rooted, dependable, and sure. Taurus is lavish and green, fecund and fertile. Let's all imagine falling back into Taurus arms and being held. Let's imagine the earth herself as those lush arms and find ourselves sprawled on our backs on nothing but green. Let's feel the touch of Taurus which is strong, firm, and kind. Let's choose to affirm our earthy solidity and the light that grows from that stable peace. Let's imagine taking our next step from that tender place.

INVITATION

Sprawl on your back on the earth and breathe. Feel the support the earth offers. If it's too cold outside, just sprawl on your living room floor and imagine the earth far beneath.

This. Here. Now.

Taurus is a great exhale. It's the perfect antidote to the thrust and assertion of Aries. While Aries pushes forth, Taurus receives. While Aries initiates, Taurus beckons. Let's remember Taurus is an internal, magnetic sign. It draws to itself the resources it needs. Taurus makes time for the beautiful in the world. It makes time to notice the ephemeral—the snowman, the violet, the last bit of the setting sun. Today, let time be on our side. Everything is better when we slow down and say—this, here, now. This morning, this breath, this listening, this pleasure, this work, this unfolding life, this unfurling self.

INVITATION

Let's use these words as a practice of presence throughout our day: "This. Here. Now." Let's allow the words to invite us to this very moment. We are often far ahead or dwelling in the past. We are rarely, oh so rarely, acknowledging the gift of this, here, now. Sometimes, when we slow the pace of our walk or our breath, this helps us arrive. Let's try using these three words to wake up to nowness.

Taurus

Think a Smile

Rest. Steep in beauty. Pause. Breathe. Sit. Meditate. Stare at the sky. Feel your feet on the earth. Walk slowly. Notice your inhale. Notice your exhale. Stop what you're doing. Pause. Notice the life you are living. Listen for your heartbeat. Notice you are not beating your own heart. Pause. Breathe deeply. Eat slowly. Drink something warm. Listen to your favorite music. Move all of your body. Smell something delicious. Wear something that feels just right. Sit, stare, breathe, write. Notice what you are feeling. Rest your head on something soft. Put down something heavy you've been carrying. Feel the plushness of the day. Pause, inhale, exhale. Think a smile. Smile.

INVITATION

Sometimes when we *think* a smile, we cannot help but smile. And when we organically smile, it opens us to receive the day in a new way. A true smile is an entrance into delight and appreciation and connection. Even when you don't feel available to the plushness of the day, try to think a smile. Feel how you soften and shift within.

Trees

Imagine a grove of trees. Let's walk through that silent grove and find a tree. First, we can marvel at its height, its presence, its staying power. Let's wrap our arms around its trunk and let our chest and cheek touch its bark. We can close our eyes and breathe and feel its roots everywhere beneath us and feel its magnificent silence. Let's sit now with our back pressed to the base of our tree. We can breathe. We can cry. We can soften. We can release. We can feel our heart held by this wisdom. We can feel this tree nourishing, filling, quenching our thirst—our thirst for stillness, silence, and timelessness. Let's stay there for a while and let our body receive the gifts of the tree that it gives always and ever freely.

INVITATION

Spend some time with a tree today. Even if you don't have time to stop and sit, simply touch the trunk as you pass. Feel the gift of its solidity and rootedness. If you have more time, listen to the tree and all it has to say.

Taurus

Slower Still

Read this small portion of a poem I wrote, slowly and out loud:

In this
mad rush
world.
We are gifted
two words.
Two little words.
I will whisper them to you.

Slower still.
Slower still,
my loves.

This excerpt is an invocation to a richer, deeper life. The pace of the world is only picking up. The mad rush is becoming madder still. Let these two little words be a beckoning for us each to live more in tune with the rhythms of the natural world.

INVITATION

How slow can you move internally today? How slow can you move externally? What do you notice when you do so? Try walking for a time at half the pace you usually walk. If you happen to be with a child, you can make it a game! If you happen to be with your child self, you can do the same!

Up and Running

There are so many delicious things to distract us, whisper to us, and intoxicate us during Taurus season. Taurus rules desire. And oh my, the list of desires is long. What tempts us? What pleases us? What pleasures us? Taurus wants in on all that action. But at some point what we once wanted so fully is no longer enticing. Our desire to grow the light within us now becomes stronger. We start to move powerfully in the direction of our aspirations. We want to overcome the lethargy, inertia, or stubbornness that prevents us from moving toward our fullest offering. We want to give of ourselves more fully. So what do we do? We rise up, dig in, and let loose. Taurus knows something about that. We can feel our strength today, our fortitude. We can get up and running.

INVITATION

Get up and run today. Start sitting at your desk or on the couch or outside on the patio and then MOVE. Run around the block. Go from complete rest to a full on charging forth. Just go for it.

Taurus

Golden Coins

Taurus rules money, coins, dollars, jewels, and valuable objects. Today, let's spend some time with money. We can go on a walk and look for pennies. We could start a piggy bank. We can search our house and collect coins under couch pillows, or in the junk drawer. We can give money away. We can organize our wallet, making a beautiful home for our money. We could also start a little fund for our next adventure. We could even ask for a raise or a loan or start a fundraising campaign. We could hang a dollar bill from a tree and let someone find it. What else could we do that would feel good and a little magical with money on this Taurean day?

INVITATION

Today, focus on organizing your wallet. Make it a beautiful place for money to land. Throw away any unnecessary papers and keep only the cards you need. Let it be beautiful and magnetizing.

Consistency

Taurus consistently shows up. And though that may sound easy, it simply isn't. It's true that if we want to build upon what we value, we often have to get physically, emotionally, or mentally stronger. To do so, we have to steadily practice. What small, consistent practice are we willing to commit to? Can we make a choice about this that would allow us to feel successful? We may just start with three deep breaths before we get out of bed each morning. Let's each consider how a certain rhythm or daily practice could improve our lives. Do we want to write? Do we want to get physically stronger? Do we want to feel less anxious? What form of repeated showing up could begin to effect change? Taurus will help us do it.

INVITATION

We will never show up with regularity and commitment if we have chosen something that requires too much time or effort immediately. So, start small. Also be sure that you are nourishing yourself in a way that allows the new commitment. It helps to tell someone too! Then you are accountable. You might even tell a friend that you will email or text once you've done your practice each day.

Gratitude

May we be grateful for this day. May we use it to take good care of ourselves and one another. May we love those we love ever more deeply and may our kindness extend its reach. May we recognize the preciousness of these lives we are living, and whisper thank you for all we may usually take for granted. May we play beautiful music, rest, eat well, and nourish ourselves and one another. May we help to grow the light. May we forgive small grievances. May we feel ourselves growing stronger—stronger in love, stronger in hope, and stronger in compassion. May we share what we have to offer. May we help each other daily. May we recognize the bounty and the goodness of this day.

INVITATION

I encourage you to read the above slowly and out loud. Don't rush through. Pause often. Feel how when you speak the word "may" out loud, it becomes an invitation. Open the door of your heart to receive and to create the day you would like to live.

Persist

We are stronger than we think we are. We all have untapped inner reserves of willpower. This is not to say we should push or over-exert and exhaust ourselves. But we must not underestimate our power to move the mountains we wish to move. Taurus is master-ful working in the rhythms of nature, the organic rhythms. It does not rush. It persists. Let's take a minute and think deeply about where we each need to persist, to continue to see something through. We can always call on Taurus to befriend us when pur-poseful power is required. Let us trust the methodical inner and outer strength of Taurus.

INVITATION

Grab a friend for this one. Ask them to stand and become a weight or obstacle to your path. Put your hands on their shoulders and push against them. Try to move them backward about ten feet (three meters). Ask your friend to resist with all their might. Not only is this fun and laughter inducing, it will also remind you just how strong you are. Sometimes when we fully physically embody persistence and power, it affects our emotional and mental capabil-ity as well.

Taurus

The Artist

Taurus rules art and beauty. Let's imagine this: We are each an artist. We can choose whatever medium we like—painting, sculpture, fabric arts, photography. Our assignment is to create a self-portrait that captures the beauty and essence of each of us. What medium would we use? What would we most hope to capture? Let's not worry about skill level. Let's imagine ourselves masterful. How would we like to capture the magnificence, the light of ourselves? What would we like to reveal? What would we like people to see?

INVITATION

Now let's not just *imagine*. Write a self-portrait in a poem. Make a collage. Make a floral bouquet. Put on great music and dance the dance of *you* today.

All Is Illumined

Taurus rules the Ajna center or the eye of intuition. The phrase for Taurus is "I see, and when the eye is opened, all is illumined." When we perceive with the inner eye, we see the light inherent in the material world. We see everything is light and everything is energy. We see the beauty that is the truth of all creation. Taurus sees the long path and walks steadily toward the light. When we are in Taurus, we can practice seeing beneath what is apparent. We can practice naming the beauty when it is not obvious. We can practice closing our eyes and opening our inner intuition. We can take a walk and feel the breeze on our skin and the sun on our face. We do not have to rush. We can receive everything that wants to offer its light to us along the way.

INVITATION

Close your eyes and put your attention at the center between your brows. Imagine this as a point of penetrating light, a light that sees into the inner worlds. Ask yourself what you see. Open the inner eye of intuition and see what it reveals. You might want to journal after this brief turning inward.

Picnic

Imagine we are all gathered around a huge patchwork, hand-made, colorful picnic blanket. We lift it to the sky and let it settle onto the grass. It's inviting. We all step from the edges onto the blanket. We carry baskets of apples, fresh bread, cheese, good books, guitars, and journals. We find the perfect spot to sit on this gorgeous, colorful expanse. First, we lie down and look at the vastness of the blue sky. We feel the nourishment of the ground at our backs. This is replenishment enough. But soon we sit up and begin to unpack our baskets. Let's imagine the food we love most is here on this blanket. The temperature is perfect. We feel quiet inside and curious. We feel hopeful. Someone reads a poem. Someone sings a song. We begin to share all the food, all the beauty, all the bounty. We offer it up. We sit together on this huge picnic blanket until the sun sets. Imagine this.

INVITATION

You guessed it: Have a picnic! An indoor picnic works too. Just spread a blanket, and feast. Maybe everyone attending brings their favorite foods to share! Let there be music. Let there be poetry. Let there be a nap. A picnic can also be a state of mind.

The Garden

In the children's book *Frog and Toad Together* by Arnold Lobel,
there's a story called "The Garden." In it, Toad wants to plant
a garden. He plants seeds and then tells the seeds to start to
grow. He paces and waits and then shouts at the ground. He
wants the seeds to grow! Frog tells Toad he may be shouting
too much, that his seeds may be afraid to grow. Frog suggests
leaving them alone for a few days. He suggests letting the sun
shine on them and letting the rain fall on them. Toad reads a
story to the seeds. He sings songs, reads poems, and plays music.
Then, finally, he is exhausted and takes a nap. When he wakes,
little green plants are coming up out of the ground, and Toad
is delighted. So, my friends, let's not shout at our hardworking
seeds. Let's sing to them instead. And when we feel most anxious, let's take a nap and let a little magic unfold.

INVITATION

Sing to what you would like to see grow! We sing to children, yes?
We sing to celebrate rites of passage. We sing sometimes to navigate a difficult hour. When we feel most thwarted or anxious or
impatient, if we can manage to sing or hum, something is released
and something softens. We cannot sing and hold on to pain.

A Salutation to the Sun

Today, let's celebrate the sun. Let's acknowledge the shining magnificence that keeps everything and everyone on this planet alive. Let's turn our faces toward the sun or do a sun salutation or feel its warmth on our skin and be thankful. We can greet the sun at dawn or acknowledge its setting. Let's remember what a miracle it is that the sun grows or warms or brightens whatever it touches. And then let's remember, something equally miraculous, that we each carry a sun at the center of our chest. It is said in fact that the heart's warmth, heat, and generosity is equal to the power of ten thousand suns. Let us truly make this a sun day and offer the blazing heat or quiet warmth of our sun hearts growing and nourishing all we touch or interact with throughout the day. We are the garden and the light that grows it.

INVITATION

Turn your face to the sun today and receive its warmth and linger in its gift. If the sun is not out today, turn your attention to the sun inside, warming you from the inside out.

What Is, Is

Sometimes Taurus feels slow, thick, and heavy. It can be hard to move. If we need to move slowly, let's move slowly. If we feel like crying for no reason, and for all the reasons, let us cry. If we need to process, digest, or let heaviness move through us, let's allow this. Truth be told, it can sometimes be hard to start the day. But it's easier when we don't rush, push, or critique. What is, is. Sometimes we must be extraordinarily gentle with the present moment. Later in the day, or even in just a few hours, we may need to call upon our strength to navigate the day. For now, let's allow whatever stillness we require. We can breathe deeply, give ourselves a little neck rub. (Taurus rules the throat and neck, after all!) Let's take some time today to be fully with our tender selves.

INVITATION

Don't rush, push, or otherwise bully yourself today. Let's remember that what is, is—until it isn't, and something new has entered. Writing is one of the greatest tools to release a feeling and welcome something new. Maybe cozy up in bed and write for 10 minutes before you emerge. Your prompt might be as simple as "I feel . . ."

Taurus

Small Delights

My great-uncle Leon was a Taurus. One of his sweetest and best qualities was his celebration of simple pleasures. Nine out of ten times, we'd be eating lunch and he would say something like, "This is the best burger I've ever had" or "This is the best ice cream sundae I've ever eaten." And he meant it each time. The Taurus energy is grateful for small daily delights. It celebrates a good meal, beautiful sunset, or a lovely walk. It appreciates the offerings of an ordinary day. It takes in the beauty and sighs with pleasure. See with Taurean eyes today—touch, savor, celebrate. Name the goodness.

INVITATION

Even if there is something to say about how a meal could be improved or an offering refined, for today, simply practice fully appreciating what is *good*. Risk hyperbole.

Sensually Alive

Taurus rules tasting, touching, seeing, hearing, smelling. Here are some delicious, sensually alive questions to ask on a Taurus day: What do you love to behold or gaze upon? What, when you see it before you, lights you up inside? What ignites or softens you when you touch it? If our hands are the extensions of our heart, what gives you the most joy to touch with your love? What sense enlivens you? What scent makes you melt? What scent reminds you of childhood? What is your favorite dessert? Your comfort food? What do you remember tasting that felt like discovery? What music has always touched you? What is the song that makes you the happiest currently? Whose voice is the most soothing for you to hear? Why? Let's name the sensory beauty!

INVITATION

Choose one or two of the questions above and write! Share your answers with a friend.

Clay

Let's imagine our hands on a potter's wheel. Let's start with the clay at the center and place our hands on its unformed density. Let's imagine that we spin the wheel and the clay begins to rise. It begins to take shape. We are bringing beauty into manifestation through our steady, careful, and consistent hands. We are finding the right speed for the wheel and the right pressure for the clay. We are neither pressing too much or too little. We are creating something beautiful and purposeful through our attention and skill. Taurus understands how to manifest. It wishes to create the beautiful. It keeps its hands on the clay and reveals the light within it.

INVITATION

What do you wish to tangibly touch and help mold? (It doesn't have to be clay.) Simply put, *make* something today. Make something beautiful.

Indigo Blue

Taurus is wine and cheese and the touch of a lover. It is indigo blue and the smell of homemade bread in the oven. It's the green grass and the trees and nature everywhere in and outside our bodies. Taurus is love poetry and hungry bodies. It is rhythm and inner quiet and all things languid. Taurus is desire. It is also unceasing light, beauty made manifest, and aspiration. It is intuition, will-in-action, and unstoppable strength. It is power incarnate and the drive to build. It is the willingness to whip the form into shape to carry the light. It is slow and steady and strong and wins the race. It is true vision. Seeing with the eye of the soul, it is patiently becoming wise. Taurus allows beauty to lead the way.

INVITATION

Make a list of three colors. Do a writing prompt for each. Start with indigo blue, the color of Taurus. What does the color awaken in you? How does it make you feel? How does it live in you? Does it invite you to think of water or midnight or a darkening sky? Let its richness invite you in.

Let Everything Good Increase in Me

Read this short poem I wrote, "Notes from My Father's Talk," slowly and out loud:

Let everything good increase in me.
Let me be teachable and live a life pledged to the
Path of Love.
May I be a steady beacon of light.
At least, let me be useful.
How can I best serve?
There is no time to lose and still I need not rush.

INVITATION

Explore the phrase "Let everything good increase in me." What if you began each day with that thought? They are words that whisper to us to allow for growth at every moment. Take a deep breath as you say these words and say them throughout the day.

What Matters Most

What do we wish to attract or accumulate? Taurus loves beautiful things and surely loves building financially, but what else? What do we value? What has meaning for us? Whenever I would ask my father what he wanted for his birthday, he would reply, "Wisdom." It's always funny and always true. What do we each value beyond the purely physical pleasures, beyond financial success? If Taurus is magnetic, what, of value, do we wish to magnetize? How can we build a life with what matters most to us? If Taurus is a garden, what are we growing? Let us actually envision the garden of our life. How does it feel to sit in this garden? If Taurus rules beauty, let us truly ask ourselves what we find beautiful. Let us build upon that and shine the great light of Taurus into our lives to grow what is precious, grow what is true.

INVITATION

Put these words at the top of your page and write for 15 minutes without stopping: "What matters most."

Our Taurus Friends

Here are the reasons it's great to have a Taurus friend:

1. They remind you to slow down and appreciate what is beautiful in life.

2. They love the natural world and will share sunsets, point out hummingbirds, and encourage you to breathe in the mountain air.

3. They are physically strong and their willpower is immense. Once they set their course, they are unstoppable.

4. They also love to relax and enjoy the goodness of life. They love to touch, taste, see, smell, and listen to all things gorgeous and delicious.

5. They manifest.

6. They can be very practical and no-nonsense. They do their work without a lot of fuss and invite you to do the same.

7. They appreciate seasons and rhythms. They trust how nature unfolds herself and they encourage you to live with the rhythms of the natural world.

8. They often sing amazingly well. They inspire with their voices.

9. They stand for, live amid, and create beauty and art.

10. They will calm you when you most need calm.

Celebrate your Taurus pals today!

INVITATION

Reach out to your Taurus pals and tell them you love them and why!

Delicious

Taurus asks us to remember what is delicious. Taurus asks us to
listen to music while we make carrot soup, to sauté onions and
dance. It invites us back into our bodies—cooking and breathing
and singing. This is the gift of the earth signs—embodiment and
full physical presence. Taurus slows us down and allows us to
appreciate the senses and the sounds and the smells of this life
we are living. May we all enjoy a little cup of carrot soup and feel
fully, deliciously nourished and cozy.

INVITATION

What's on the menu tonight? Do you have time to browse through
a cookbook before you decide? Can you take your time making a
meal? Can you cook with someone you like? Enjoy the process!

Taurus

Stillness

Let's practice becoming still. My friend once stood so still that birds came to feed from his hand. Exquisite stillness brought exquisite gifts. Let's invite our mind to rest. Let's put our quiet, calm hands on our body and breathe stability. So often we are running and our thoughts are ten steps ahead of our patient body. Stillness invites presence. Presence invites appreciation and love. Love heals all pain. When we welcome stillness, we begin to be one with the rhythms of nature, with the beating of our own heart, with time gently passing. We become the loving observer and the one entirely present. Today, let's give ourselves the gift of stillness.

INVITATION

Find someplace beautiful to sit for a time. Or keep it simple and sit on your own couch. But choose stillness for 10 minutes. You can keep your eyes open or closed. Just be still. Notice how heightened all your senses become in the stillness.

Hum

Let's hum. Yes, that's right. The minute you finish reading this, just start to hum. Make up a melody. Hum your favorite childhood lullaby. Hum a song you've always loved and yes, really commit to it. Why? Taurus rules the whole throat center. It rules the singing voice. It rules beauty and calm. Humming is something we often find ourselves doing when we are relaxed and content. Let's invoke that inner quiet and sense of peace. Humming invites us to take deep breaths to support the sound. It slows us down. It's soothing and it gets us out of our heads.

INVITATION

Ready, set, hum (or sing!). Let there be a melody in your day today—one that you create.

Taurus

Light

Taurus is the sign of light. Let's do a simple exercise. Let's close our eyes and imagine a light at the center of our chest. Let's allow it to grow, fill our body, and then break through the skin. Let it grow and extend outward like a sun. We can extend that light as far as we are able. Let it shine into our home, our city, our country, the planet. Now we can breathe and gently let that go. Now let us imagine we have the ability to see deeply into all things. Let's see the light within every form. Let's see the light in each person. See how the light varies. Practice. Now we can offer our light to another in our life that needs that gift. Let's feel how so many of us at this moment are offering our light across distance to others who soak it in. Know that all of these exercises tangibly make this world better. Let the illumination of Taurus fill you. Let it fill you up. Let it spill out to all you meet.

INVITATION

How is the light where you live? Does your house need some illumination? It makes a difference. Buy an extra lamp. Change a light bulb. Brighten up, inside and out.

Something Is Growing

Let's imagine this together. We are each sitting on a bench somewhere outdoors. Next to us, a little seedling begins to sprout,
cracking through the earth, making its presence known. Here are
some questions about our seedling.

1. What is sprouting? Is it a flower, tree, or something
    else entirely?

2. What color is it?

3. Let's say as it unfurls, it presents us with a word or
    a sound or a feeling of something that is growing
    in us this year. What is the word? The sound, the
    feeling?

4. How do you feel about this little seedling growing
    next to you?

5. Does it have a name? Taurus asks us to remember
    that under all the agitation and sometimes turmoil
    in our lives, something is growing and it's good to
    notice.

INVITATION

Do not limit yourself in this visualization. An exotic flower may be
growing. Or maybe it's not even plant life. Maybe it's a person.
Maybe it's a lake. Maybe it's a path that beckons. Your seedling
could become almost anything.

Welcoming Gemini

We welcome the month of Gemini. Gemini is a an outgoing sign full of movement and intelligence. We connect, converse, circulate, and exchange. We collect facts. We tell our stories. Gemini rules how we think, write, and speak. We offer our message to the world and look for a response. We become messengers for what we most value or love. Gemini is primarily a sign of relationship and goodwill. The drive is to connect and weave a tapestry of relationship that reveals the connection of everyone and everything. We create conversation to broaden consciousness. We all can feel the difference between polite conversation and a true meeting of hearts and minds. It is a kind of communion and not just a conversation. We exchange ideas to build true wisdom. The greatest opportunity of this month is to cultivate conversation with the true you. Refuse to see superficially. Then, look deeper at every encounter, at every exchange. Refuse to polarize. Our hearts can blaze with oneness.

INVITATION

If you don't have a journal yet, now is definitely the time to get one! Gemini is the month of writing. Grab some stationery while you are at it! Gemini loves to write letters.

Writing Practice

Gemini carries the power of the written word. So, this month is a perfect time to begin a daily writing practice. When we write, we give form to our inner life. We see ourselves on the page. We overhear ourselves. We hold up a mirror to the dance within. This month, I'll be sharing a lot of writing prompts for you to explore. Here are a few that might spark you to begin:

> *What songs do you like to sing when you are alone in your car and driving for miles?*
>
> *Tell me about a time you simply could not stop laughing.*
>
> *Tell me about a time you cried for hours.*
>
> *When do you feel most generous?*

INVITATION

Choose one of these prompts and write! Dare yourself to share it with a friend when you are done. Or find a friend that will be your writing partner for the rest of the year!

Three Messages

Let's close our eyes and imagine we reach both hands out in front of us to greet someone. Who appears? What do they have to say to us? What message do they deliver? Let us thank them. Keeping our eyes closed, let's imagine we extend our arms again to welcome our next messenger. Who is there? What are their words for us? Let's thank them. And a third time, let's allow ourselves to be surprised. Who has a message for us? Let's feel gratitude and notice who appeared. Let's feel the lines of light that connect us with each of these three.

INVITATION

If you feel so called, write down the messages received. Is there anything that connects the three messengers? Is there a common theme? How do you feel different after receiving these words? If you prefer, work with just one messenger and listen deeply.

Gemini

Our Gemini Friends

Today, let us celebrate our Gemini friends. Here are the reasons it's great to have a Gemini friend:

1. They are amazing connectors. If you need a handyman, chiropractor, tutor, or nanny, they have a number for you immediately.

2. They are curious, bright, youthful, and inspire us all to learn and educate ourselves.

3. They can talk with anyone about anything and often get the conversation started.

4. They love you by connecting you with what you need most.

5. They are light and funny, with a great sense of humor.

6. They know the facts. Your Gemini friend will always know what you need to know and if they don't, they will find out.

7. They have a childlike wonder about the world and are often great with kids.

8. They are amazing multitaskers.

9. They leave goodwill in their wake. They like to forge positive, loving relationships.

10. They love to write letters or emails or texts and will definitely stay in touch.

Hurrah for sweet Geminis!

INVITATION

Reach out and connect with your Gemini pals to tell them you love them and why!

Our Hands

Today, let's pay attention to our hands. Gemini rules, among other things, the hands, arms, and lungs. But today let's focus on our hands. Let's remember that our hands are an extension of the heart. They are like paintbrushes for the energy of the heart. What will we touch? Whom will we touch? How will we touch? Let's notice what we do with our hands all day. Are we wringing our hands, biting our nails, brushing our own or our children's hair? Are we appreciating all that hands can do? Let's notice when we use our hands to give and when we use our hands to receive. Let's notice the myriad ways hands are a blessing. Today, we pay attention to how we touch the world with love.

INVITATION

Notice your hands today. Notice all they do. And if you feel called to do so, write about your hands. You might also write about your father's hands, your mother's hands, or your lover's hands.

Gemini

Love Languages

Gemini rules language and loving connection. What is your language of love, my friends? By all means, speak it today. Sing it. Shout it. Touch with it. Bake. Run. Walk. Reach out and change someone's day with your language of love. Stand on a street corner and hand out flowers. Say "Hello, love" to everyone you meet. Let love pour through your gaze. Do not let a pair of lonely eyes pass you by. Offer simple gestures of love: Hold open the door. Say a warm hello. Laugh with a stranger. There is always time for love. Make a room brighter by sitting in it. Leave love in your wake. Remind others just how lovable they are. If you feel lonely, offer your wide love to the sky, to a puppy, to the barista. Offer the softness of yourself. Receive the kindness of another. Let's make it our mission to use all the languages of love. Today, let's work a little magic. Let's skyrocket the love meter.

INVITATION

Practice simple gestures of love. Also practice *noticing* acts of love given and received. Name them love. Feel grateful for them.

Inviting Stillness

The pace generally picks up during Gemini season, but let's see if we can avoid the sometimes heightened anxiety. It's extra import-ant to consciously take deep breaths—breaths that check in with the whole body and not just the buzz of the brain. It's easy to get caught up in mental loops that deplete us. Instead, let's stop throughout the day, put our hand on our heart or belly, and allow for stillness. Sometimes we can quietly ask questions of our-selves that nourish, replenish, and fortify. We might ask, "What do I need to do to feel more available at this moment?" Or, "What small action might feel relieving? How can I release or relax a bit more in this moment?" Or, we might simply sigh and whisper, "Shhhh." We might ask, "Am I overexerting?" Or, "What kind thing might I say to myself right now?"

INVITATION

Take three deep breaths. Make a tiny adjustment in your body that allows you to feel quieter inside. What do you know that consis-tently helps you feel more *still* inside? Let's choose to reset again and again.

Self and Self

We are currently living in a world of great divides—one in which we need wise and loving thought and action to bridge the duality. Every day and with increased intensity, we feel the play of apparent opposites in our world. You are this. I am that. Never will we meet. We must find a way to speak the language of our inherent oneness. We can begin to know and feel in our daily practice *self* and *self*, not *self* and *other*. Gemini invites us to find the language that connects, weaves, understands, and articulates common ground. We can ask this every day: What is the common ground I share with you? And you? And you?

INVITATION

Today, dig a little deeper into the realm of our shared humanity. Go to a public space, look out at a stranger or two, and reflect on possible common ground. It's easy to quickly judge or dismiss, to relegate another to "not like me." But what about our sameness?

Courageous Conversations

What does "courageous conversation" mean to you? When is the last time you had a conversation that required a ton of courage? Have there been times you dared to speak and, because you dared, you made a big difference or impact? How have you found the courage to speak when you knew you needed to? What can we say to one another that will help us each dare to bring more of that courage, that fire of the heart, to our daily communication? Often life requires huge courage and loving fortitude. Let us uplift one another.

INVITATION

Put your attention on your heart. Take a few deep breaths. What does your heart want to say? Speak it—even if you are alone. Courageously listen. And then, see if there is someone with whom you could share what you hear.

Gemini

Both/And

Gemini rules two-ness. It is *both/and*. It is *either/or*. It's "I changed my mind" and "I changed my mind again." Gemini says, "I'm not one thing." Sometimes, with Gemini, we are asked to hold a paradox. I'm sad *and* inspired. I'm tired and motivated. I'm mad and in love. I love my life and I'm restless. I'm crazy smart and hopelessly naïve. I want to grow my work and I'm ready to walk away from it all. When we can hold paradox, we soften. We forgive ourselves a little when two wildly different self-descriptions are both true.

INVITATION

Let's explore the two-ness of Gemini, the *both/and*. Let's explore the opposites. So today let's choose one of these writing exploration pairs and write for 10 minutes about each. You could explore all of them over this week. If you like, take the time to dive deep with each pair:

1. I love / I don't love

2. I want to tell you / I don't want to tell you

3. I feel guilty about / I feel proud of

4. I feel tired when / I feel alive when

We carry many paradoxes within. And holding the truth of both makes us more complex and interesting humans.

Kind Words

What is the kindest, most loving thing you can say to yourself right now? Stop before you even finish reading this and say it out loud. Another way to ask the same question is, "What would the kindest parents say to you about yourself right now?" Take a breath and dare yourself to answer without qualification. Gemini is a sign of intelligent love. We can speak to ourselves soulfully. We can address our struggling selves with love. We can name growth. Will you whisper those words to yourself, those kind, loving words?

INVITATION

Truly. Dare yourself to say a few kind things about yourself right now. Whisper them. Speak them. Sound them forth.

Gemini

So Many Questions

Grab a pen and meet me on the page. You can choose any one of these prompts and write for 10 minutes. Or you can quickly answer them all:

Tell me about the sky right now.

Tell me how she broke your heart.

Tell me what he said before he left.

What keeps you awake at night?

In what ways do you feel young?

In what ways old?

Where and how do you feel tender right now?

INVITATION

Maybe not today but soon, go back through your writing from today or prompts you've written from this book and underline any sections that feel particularly juicy. When you are next ready to write, use one of the lines you wrote today as a prompt for your next writing session. In this way, we go deeper. We peel away layers. We get to the heart of the matter.

Siblings

Gemini rules siblings. On a Gemini day, call your brother. Call your
sister. Talk about everything and nothing. Feel the sweetness
and the ache of how much we have to offer one another, how our
differences help us grow, how a simple connected conversation
can set us right. Let's ask our siblings or our chosen sisters and
brothers about new dreams they are holding. Let's meet them
afresh. We might even ask them for reflections they hold about
us. What have they noticed about how we are living our lives?
Let's be curious about those we think we know best.

INVITATION

When is the last time you sent your sibling a letter, a real letter? Or
a card? Maybe today is the day.

Meditate

Here is a little five minute Gemini meditation. Let's close our eyes and put our hands on our hearts. Let's allow names and faces from our entire life to appear before us. Let's feel a line of light directly from our heart to each person who shows up. Let's remember our friend from fifth grade, our uncle, a teacher whose name we forget but who awakened our young mind or heart. Let's keep drawing lines of light until our heart has multiple beams connected to others. Let's also extend lines of light to faces and hearts we don't know yet, but will soon. And let's take a moment to envision everyone else with multiple streams of light coming from their own hearts. Let's breathe together. We can build a world of loving connection.

INVITATION

Put the book down and spend 5 minutes in meditation. This is the moment. Don't delay.

Young and Bright

Gemini does not hesitate to say, "Who are you and what do you do? And what do you love, and why?" It wants to talk. When in Gemini, we can invite inner conversation as well. We can greet ourselves with delight. "Hello, old pal!" And then, we can ask ourselves how we'd like to spend the day. If we happen to respond, "Well, how do you think? I'm headed off to work for ten hours." Then let's ask ourselves if there's any way to bring a little joy into the equation. "Self," we can say, "I have a few ideas to spice things up. Let's stop and get a fancy coffee or sing on the way to work or let's wear fabulous red shoes." Let's call on the invention and spontaneity of our child selves and simply say yes to their suggestions. Let's invite someone to lunch or invite someone to collaborate in any way. We can keep it light and lively.

INVITATION

What choices can you make today that feel young and bright? How might you follow your curiosity in playful ways?

Gemini

Asking New Questions

Sometimes after gathering with family or dear friends, we realize we didn't ask the questions or have the conversations we wish we'd had. Sometimes old patterns of silence take over or we skim the surface and never fully dive in. When in Gemini, it's a perfect time to connect and ask new questions of loved ones. Today, let's talk about the future—about hopes and dreams, plans and visions. Let's allow ourselves to be surprised. We can meet a loved one anew. We can ask questions we think we know the answer to but stay open to the unexpected. It's OK to feel uncomfortable at first. Let's talk about what matters most to us and invite others to engage. Let's carve out new territory with old friends and family.

INVITATION

What is something you don't know or remember about a loved one? Dismiss small talk and ask them interesting and new questions today.

Hello, Friend

Gemini is a sign of goodwill. Goodwill includes friendliness, cooperation, or helpfulness. So much is possible with a dose of friendliness. Cooperation is lifesaving and seems to be a dying art. Gemini reminds us that everything is so much easier and more joyful if we sprinkle a little helpfulness and kindness into the equation. Gemini calls upon its soul-centered ruler, Venus, to unite apparent dualities or opposites. Venus loves to fuse, blend, and forge loving relationships. And Gemini often does this through conversation. It invites anyone and everyone to have a chat. Gemini says, once we've chatted, we are connected and connection is my joy. Today, let's walk in our day with a will to do good.

INVITATION

Strike up a conversation today while you are waiting in line. Compliment someone out of the blue. Talk to someone on the elevator. Say hello to someone you pass on your walk, but make it a warm hello. Connect!

Gemini

Refuse Jaded

Gemini wants, above all else, to feel engaged. It loves the exchange of words and lively conversation. It is butterfly energy, touching this flower and that one, curious and ever-moving. Gemini gets around, enlivening everyone en route. When in Gemini, we have the opportunity to heartfully connect and to exchange ideas. We have a chance to be heard and for our message and our thoughts to be received. We can use Gemini to invite. We can use Gemini to delight. Let's welcome vibrant. Let's refuse jaded and instead get curious. We can learn something new today. We can walk with a bit of wonder. Let's refuse "Same old, same old" and invite sparkle and verve. Gemini is young at heart and willing. Where should we go? Who will we see? What will we talk about? What can we learn? What unexpected delights might cross our path? Let's get curious.

INVITATION

Curiosity keeps us young. What are you curious about today? How might you explore the question you are holding? Does it require a phone call? Or some research? Would a good independent bookstore hold the key to your question? Follow the curiosity and see where it leads.

Your Secret Name

It's time to write! Here are some questions. Choose one that speaks to you most deeply or write a little about them all. Are you game? Let's go.

> *What is your secret name?*
>
> *What is your greatest superpower?*
>
> *What makes you feel most soft?*
>
> *What do you long for?*
>
> *What part of your body needs the most love right now?*
>
> *Who knows you best and why?*
>
> *What are you carrying that it's time to put down?*

INVITATION

If you feel like it, work with your secret name over the upcoming week. Say hello to yourself as that name as the day begins. See how your secret name makes you feel when you try it on for the day.

Gemini

What No Longer Fits

Let's find words to name our discomfort or frustration. What no longer fits? We have to name it, sit with it, and eventually act on it. Gemini finds the words that fit the pain or passion. What is rumbling inside each of us? Can we find powerful words that do not attack but rather insist on action and change? There are inner words and outer words, ways we talk to ourselves and ways we work with others. Let's not be thwarted but instead catalyzed by precisely naming our closures or blockages. Therein freedom lies.

INVITATION

Use this writing prompt: "What no longer fits."

Quality

Gemini converses, chats, podcasts, and tweets. Under Gemini, we talk to ourselves. We talk to everyone else. We email. It is often nonstop and too much. The speed of it all can be bewildering. We are, of course, more connected today than at any other time in history. But Gemini at its best asks us to consider the quality of that connection. It also asks us to stop and make sure our inner communication isn't too chaotic. Silence and breath help calm the inner noise. Sometimes, under Gemini, we have to step away from all the exchanges, center ourselves, and reemerge with clarity about who we truly need to talk to and what we truly need to say.

INVITATION

You may need to make a plan for this one! Spend a day in as much silence as possible. If you can pull it off, spend the entire day in silence.

Gemini

Child Streak

The musical artist Prince was a Gemini and often talked about his "child streak." There is a bit of Peter Pan in anyone with strong Gemini in their chart. In fact, many people with a lot of Gemini end up choosing not to have children of their own as their own child streak is so strong. There is a gift in the youthfulness of Gemini. It allows us all to feel closer to our own child self—and that child self's needs, wants, yearnings, and fears. On a Gemini day, let's allow our young selves to come along for the ride.

INVITATION

Try to find a few moments today when your child self gets to take the lead. Where does your child self want to eat lunch? How does your child self want to walk to work?

The Power of the Word

Words hold healing power. Every time we speak, we have the chance to add light to a relationship, a family, a community, or even to humanity. The words we choose leave a quality of energy in their wake. Gemini says, "Use your words for good. Use your words to heal. Use your words to promote love. Use your words—the power of language and communication—to bring fundamental change." Let us practice consciously communicating. Let us realize we are building our actual world every time we speak. The power of the word is strong. Sometimes one tiny yes can turn our world around. Sometimes one message of encouragement can change the entire course of a day. Let's all use our words in the name of support and evolution and compassion. Let's use our words to grow the light.

INVITATION

Today, I simply ask that you notice how your words land. Are they uplifting? Are they encouraging? Are they penetrating? Are they instructive? Helpful? What power are you putting out into the world through your choice of words?

Gemini

The Shape of Our Loss

Let's write. If you prefer to stop and dive in with the first question, feel free to disregard the rest. See which questions wake something up inside you and demand an answer:

1. What is ripe in you and what is dying?

2. What do your hands know?

3. What part of your body wants fuller expression?

4. What are the greatest losses you have lived through? How have they changed you?

5. What is the shape of your loss? Is there any part of you more alive after the loss?

6. Which appointment were you born to keep?

INVITATION

There's a coffee shop in Los Angeles where people leave their writing tucked in drawers at the tables where customers sit. You can sit and read the musings and pain and love of hundreds of customers. Take one of your answers today and leave it in a place that someone might happen upon it and be touched or inspired to write themselves.

The Lungs

Gemini rules the lungs. Let's use the following as a kind of meditation: Let's begin with an exhale. Together, let's breathe in *quiet* and breathe out *fear*. Let's breathe in *health* and breathe out *anxiety*. Let's breathe in *connection* and breathe out *isolation*. Let's breathe in *spaciousness* and breathe out *worry*. Breathe in *stillness* and breathe out *self-doubt*. Let's breathe in the power to *transform* and breathe out *powerlessness*. And then, dear friends, let's simply breathe.

INVITATION

Choose one set of words from the meditation above. Deepen the invitation and release with each breath. Read the poem "Blessing of Breathing" by Jan Richardson and focus on your own breathing.

The Hands We've Held

Let's think about all the hands we've held. Really. Let's stop a minute and think about all those hands—our mother's, father's, friend's, lover's, children's hands. How did all those different hands feel in yours? And let's think of all whom we've greeted with our hands, all the hellos and goodbyes, all the "I see you and thank-yous." And now, let's think simply about this: To whom would you like to offer an open hand? And, if you like, let's open our hands now and offer them as a gesture of willingness and growth, friendship, and acceptance.

INVITATION

Today, remember that the hands are an extension of the heart and again, notice what you do with your hands throughout the day. How do you treat your hands and whom do you touch?

Messenger

Whom or what do we speak for? Whom or what are we a messenger for in the world? It doesn't have to be one thing forever. It's good to ask ourselves what we speak for with our whole heart. Let's try to answer this. It can be totally imperfect. Perhaps we speak for the protection of animals. Perhaps we speak for the power of love and dissolving fear. Perhaps we speak for evolving our consciousness around how we treat and care for one another or for those who cannot currently speak for themselves. Let's spend some time together thinking about our messenger selves.

INVITATION

Use this writing prompt: "I am a messenger for . . . "

JUNE 16

Gemini

Reading and Writing

Gemini rules the written word. Who is one of your favorite writers? Why? Can you articulate the gift you receive reading their work? Reading great writing is such an intimate, life-changing experience. It broadens our world, names our fragility, inspires, encourages, cracks our heart open, and then mends it, makes us laugh. It's deep nourishment. When we find a writer we love, sometimes we read everything they've written. We want to understand their unfolding, artistic journey. We want to steep in their particular wisdom. Gemini is also a great connector. So, let's connect one another with the writers we love. I realize I'm drawn to writers who share deep vulnerability, who demonstrate the power to walk any burning ground, and who possess the ability to truly celebrate life. Who are your absolute favorites, or what is one book that you truly feel changed the course of your life?

INVITATION

Share a favorite book with three favorite friends. Lend or send them a copy. Say, "Read this!"

Reduce Distraction

Gemini can get very distracted, but distraction does not have to win the day. I invite us to listen deeply today. We can start with our breath. Then we can listen outward. We can listen to leaves, rustling, birdsong, water lapping, laughter just outside the window, bikers riding past. We can get quiet enough inwardly to receive. Receive the day and let the day organically unfold. Don't overdo it. Don't try to take on too much. Let's do our best not to multi-task. Let's put our full attention on one thing, and then another.

INVITATION

Listening beyond our usual sphere of attention is a beautiful way to calm the nervous system. We can listen for the ocean even if we could never hear it. But we could also listen for the birdsong that may be in the neighbor's yard. Listen beyond the click of computer keys and the hum of the dryer. What do you hear? And how do you feel while listening?

Do Two Things

Gemini says, "Sometimes if you want to get something done, do two things." Gemini thrives with a little back and forth. It needs to move. So, if you have a deadline for a project, work on the project but also make soup. OR if you've promised yourself you are going to write all day, WRITE, but also take several walks around the block. Gemini loves variety. Don't confine yourself to any one thing. Do what you need to do but give yourself wiggle room to keep it all lively and interesting.

INVITATION

What are the two things you might do in tandem today?

The Dance of Gemini and Cancer

Have you started to notice the in-breath and out-breath of the signs? Every sign has an external or internal polarity, and they alternate. We are now moving toward the sign Cancer when the activity, movement, and exchange of Gemini gives way to the quiet inner currents. When we cross the threshold into Cancer, we enter the realm of feeling. We leave behind the intense mental focus and rapid movement of Gemini and feel our way forward. The relationships and connections we forge in Gemini deepen and are nourished in Cancer. Cancer always asks that we return home to ourselves. We feel deeply outward and deeply inward. We might even silently begin to give form to some of what we thought about under Gemini. Cancer knows how to gestate and nourish an idea so it grows to fruition and can be birthed.

INVITATION

Today, use the energy of Gemini to write about Cancer themes. Ask yourself, "What is home?" Stretch beyond your usual definitions. Maybe home is your physical house, or maybe it's your beating heart. Maybe it's your mother's hands. Maybe home is the presence of a beloved teacher or a piece of music sung by a child. What is home for you?

Cancer

Welcoming Cancer

The sign Cancer, at its best, is the most profound mothering energy around. It holds, enfolds, listens, and feeds. It comforts and soothes the pain. There is something vast and spacious in how people with strong Cancer energy listen and receive. They need not say a word and yet one is generously fed. We can all steep in this energy during the Cancerian month. There is nothing passive about Cancer. The energy is potent. It is the energy of a creative builder. It is the sign of birth. It brings the new to life with awesome care and protection. The only caveat for the month of Cancer is to focus on sharing your emotional responses as they emerge and not stuffing down disappointment or hiding resentment. There can be a tendency to nurse wounds and close down instead of addressing hurt or disappointment in the moment. So, during this next month, breathe your way forward. Fill your belly with breath, good food, and self-compassion. Choose to put your full mama-loving (or papa-loving) nourishment on something and whisper to it or just listen to it. Watch it flourish in your tender care.

INVITATION

Today, reflect on all the projects from the month of Gemini. Gemini called us out into the world. Now is the time to call our energy inward and quietly begin to brew or gestate an idea. Sit for a moment and allow yourself to release all outer activity. Feel something new growing within.

Cancer

Homecoming

Cancer rules homecoming—the home that is our body, the home that is our very self. So much calls us away, wrenches us from the seat at the center of who we are. Every day we must return home again and again—the home that is our breath, the home that is our beating heart. We must befriend the tender corners, the need for rest. We must accept and include the chaos of living as a part of the hearth and home we are. The sign Cancer is a refuge, a heart home, a deep well of nourishment. May we offer this to one another. Maybe we remember our tenderness. May we embody home.

INVITATION

Let's start simple. Place one hand on your belly and one hand on your heart, and take at least three deep breaths. Quietly say to yourself, "I am home" or, "Welcome home. All feelings are welcome here."

Raw

The ongoing question for Cancer is this: Do I protect myself from possible pain or do I show up as vulnerable and emotionally naked as I feel? It is difficult to navigate the sensitivity of this sign. There's often the feeling that one could be hurt or rejected at any time. Cancer says, "shouldn't we just anticipate this and protect ourselves?" Sometimes Cancer says, "and shouldn't I protect you too?" When in Cancer, we can all feel a bit raw. We might be more reactive than usual, or we might not even risk interaction and stay home. We all grow under the Cancer energy when we say "Let's risk it. Let's risk being emotionally real with one another." It's scary, but also sometimes exhilarating. We'll just tell the vulnerable, sometimes messy or awkward truths, shed a few tears, and then maybe we can bake a delicious chocolate cake and have a little party. What say you? Cancer invites us to be feelingly alive and dares us to be intimate with our sensitivity.

INVITATION

Let's physically open our bodies. Uncross your arms and legs and let your arms rest at your sides. Practice being physically available. This cannot help but inspire emotional availability and vulnerability as well.

Cancer

The Soft Places

Cancer rules the stomach and the breasts. Both of these areas are tender, sensitive, and ever changing. Those with strong Cancer energy in their charts love to nourish, feed, and tend to those that need tending. They give of their bodies, energy, and vitality to make sure we are all fed physically, emotionally, and mentally or spiritually. And simultaneously, they often digest and assimilate so much of the pain of the world. They feel everything and eat the darkness so we can live in the light. It's fundamental, however, that those with strong Cancerian energy practice not absorbing the pain, but out shining it with light so they don't carry it. We can all work to help nourish those in need. We can all practice letting light illuminate the darkness through our nonreactivity, presence, and fierce love.

INVITATION

Take a moment and notice the front surface of your body. Notice the chest and the stomach. Notice how it feels to cross your arms in front of your chest and protect and notice how it feels to stand more exposed. Notice how it feels to focus on softening the front surface of your body, rendering it more receptive. Observe this throughout the day.

The Voice of the Body

Cancer is a sign deeply connected to the body and to the stories our bodies tell. So we ask: What do our bodies want and need to say? What are they holding that seeks release? What secrets are stored in the body's silence? Sometimes we numb the body by ignoring its needs. Sometimes we liberate it into fuller joy by listening. Today, let's ask ourselves what our bodies are yearning to reveal. Let's give our bodies a voice. What wants to be born through us? How can we allow our physical bodies to experience more light? Sometimes pain must speak to carve out a river where joy can flow.

INVITATION

Let's write. Ask yourself: What does my body need to say? (Hint: You might try writing with your nondominant hand for 5 to 10 minutes. It feels awkward but reveals truths!) Don't edit or judge what you've written. Instead, bear witness to your own need and fragility or your own strength and vitality. When you are done, place your hand on your heart, brow, or belly, and offer your body love. One touch can be like spoken gratitude. Our own touch is a direct line to kindness and relief.

Cancer

Suddenly Spinning

The sign of Cancer can be quite emotionally intense. We might be going about our day and then have one tiny comment, email or sudden memory send us spinning. And often our reaction feels huge in comparison to what sparked it. We all experience the ever-changing tides of Cancerian energy. Today, I would offer these suggestions:

1. Try not to take it personally.
2. It's probably not as bad as you currently feel it to be.
3. Try to clarify what is under the first layer of feeling.
4. Try to express that feeling clearly and thoughtfully, without apology or blame.

Our invitation is to navigate the ocean of feeling with breath, calm, and perspective.

INVITATION

Think back to something that recently sent you spinning. Can you detach a bit from the immediate emotional reactivity and feel what might be under that reaction? Was it the event or person that sent you spinning or was it something from your past that acted as a trigger? We have to become the observers of our lives so we can learn to make different and better choices as we grow.

Come In, Come In

The soul-centered phrase for Cancer is "I build a lighted house and therein dwell." Let's think about all the many forms of a lighted house. Yes, certainly it's our physical body, but it is also our emotional body, our mental body, and our entire personality. We are here to build our house of light. And of course our lighted house can be built outside ourselves as well. Is our lighted house an art gallery, a production company, a boxing gym? Is our lighted house our growing family? Let's think about what it is to build something as well. Sometimes building is very practical. We build a brick-and-mortar business or a family home. But sometimes it's much subtler. What is the quality of our thought? How do we work with our emotions? This too is a kind of building. It's an invitation and an opportunity. Let's all build a lighted house of our own body, our home, our family, our community, and our planet. Every day with each tiny choice, let's grow the light.

INVITATION

I'm going to invite your inner fourth grader to draw "a lighted house." And then I'm going to invite your inner proud parent to hang it on the wall. Let's remind ourselves that we are always working to build and live in a house of light.

Cancer

Nest

Suggestions for a Cancerian day:

1. Feel your feelings.

2. Give yourself some alone time.

3. If you are having crinkly feelings, make a pot of soup or bake a pie or stretch or punch a punching bag.

4. Don't hide.

5. Tell somebody what you feel. That always helps.

6. A good soundtrack and a soft blanket also help.

7. Do something in your home that makes it feel even lovelier or more cozy.

8. Invite friends into your lighted house for pie.

9. That's right. Do not eat pie alone.

INVITATION

Let's work on number 7 in this list. What is something you could do in your home that would allow your pleasure, joy, or calm to increase when you are there? Maybe you could clean a corner and sort through a few piles. Maybe you could make a little altar. Maybe you could clean the kitchen and make a pie!

Softening

Let's close our eyes. Even now, let's slow our breathing and let our forehead relax—our jaw, our throat. Let's allow our chest to soften, allow our belly to be as it is. Let's allow the front surface of our body to soften. Then we can imagine we are standing in the light of day. The sun is overhead. We can feel the sun on our skin. We feel what we feel. We let our breath nourish us. We don't curl in or protect the softness. We let this softness be a superpower. Let's stay open to receive. Let's stay open to be touched. Walk in. Let's walk into our day, willing not to close. We are always only doing one of two things— opening to love or closing down around it.

INVITATION

Check in with yourself several times today and simply ask: Am I opening to love? Or am I closing down around it? How could I open to the love of this moment?

Cancer

Raucous Light

Sometimes, steeped in the Cancerian energy, we find ourselves revisiting past hurts or nursing old resentments. We tell ourselves the story of how we've been wronged. We carry that resentment or hurt or wound like a stone in our pocket. We rub this stone. We grip it. We don't let go. It begins to define a part of our daily living. Now let's imagine we take that stone out of our pocket and place it in our palm. We see it from every angle. We ask ourselves how it has felt to carry this. Then if we so choose, we take a deep breath and we fling that stone into a great wide ocean of forgiveness and love. We no longer have to carry something that does not contribute to our joy. Something new begins to surface in us. As we detach, new freedom emerges. As we extricate ourselves from resentment or disappointment, the past will not define our next steps forward. We can now welcome the unexpected and delightful. We've made room for something truly new to enter. Let's all practice cleaning our Cancerian houses, making room for raucous light.

INVITATION

Let's use this writing prompt: "I will no longer carry . . ."

One Little Light

Have you ever taken a walk at night and passed houses with one room alight, casting a glow of comfort? One little light in a window is so inviting. Many little lights across the world and throughout time have beckoned, welcomed, and sometimes saved us—the lighthouse, the campfire, the candle in the cabin window that says, "I am here." When we are lost, we search for light. When the night is long, we wait for the first signs of dawn. We are all here to build and intensify the light we are. Better yet, we are here to be the beacon in a storm for another, to be the warm campfire providing nourishment, to be the lighted heart and hearth that says, "Come in, love. Come in. You are safe now. It is warm here. Come in." This is a day for inclusivity and warmth.

INVITATION

Today, light a candle. As you light it, imagine the flame at the center of your chest. Feel your body as a house of light. Watch the candle flame and remember that the light of the heart is lit throughout our lives. It never goes out, no matter how dark the hour, no matter how dim the light becomes. Then, as a practice, let the light grow. Let it become a full flame. Let it become the sun. Let it grow until it illuminates your entire being. Now, imagine someone you love or something that needs your love and welcome them, in your imagination, into your lighted house. Feel how your light can nourish, tend to, and uplift another.

Cancer

Feeling-Sensitivity

The journey for Cancer is from moodiness to *"feeling-sensitivity."* Our moods can take over our inner house and run rampant, leaving destruction in our wake. We don't want to stuff the feeling into a downstairs closet but we also don't want the mood to win the day. When we are feelingly-sensitive, we pay attention. We offer compassion to ourselves and others. When feeling-sensitivity works with a mood, it says, "I see you. I feel you. I see your pain. I feel your fear. If you need to go outside and run around the block, go for it. Or if you need to go yell in your car, you can do that too. Otherwise, just lay your head on my lap and I will soothe you. You are just fear becoming love."

INVITATION

First, let's list our feeling state. How do you feel right now? List everything—the good, the bad, and the ugly. Write it or say it out loud. Now close your eyes and deepen your breathing. Let your forehead relax. So too, your jaw, your throat. Allow your chest to soften. Let your belly be as it is. Let one of your moods step forward, present itself. Then, whisper or think, "I set you free." Say it as many times as you need to. You might even need to let the mood dance. Move your body as you say, "I set you free." Embodiment releases the pressure. Let your breath help the release. Let your softness be a superpower. Let your willingness to let go be the practice of today. Use your feeling-sensitivity to keep listening to what you need next to release in a compassionate, full way.

Loving Waters

This is a blessing for what feels fragile in our lives. May these words be a balm, a comfort, a reminder that our story is always unfolding. Fragility can grow powerful wings. Shame learns to breathe in the light of day. Tender places are soothed with loving touch and time. Even when we feel numb or fragile, blood is pumping and air is circulating and our hearts are beating out the invitation to our next tiny steps. Let's tend to our own fragility with curiosity and kindness. Let's rock ourselves—not to sleep, but into aliveness and awakening. May this blessing be like a summer thunderstorm that beckons us out to get soaked in its loving waters.

INVITATION

Write about a thunderstorm you've experienced. Have you ever stood out in the rain? Have you ever gotten soaked by a summer shower? Write about how it felt.

Cancer

Good Job

Let's remember that we are alive and tender. We are feeling, yearning, and loving. We are oh so human—full of desire and pain, full of uncertainties and strength. We are working to make good decisions and truly doing the best we can. We are working to be positive and resilient and striving to be good daughters and sons, good husbands and wives, good employees, good bosses. We want to grow. We are loving what we've chosen to love. And we are practicing widening that circle. We are summoning courage to take our next big leap. We are doing our best to care for our bodies, to elevate our feeling life, to improve our inner monologues. We are making plans. We are practicing staying present. We are teaching ourselves new skills. We are always starting again. We are growing our strength. We are offering our friendship. We are celebrating others. We are doing a good job, friends. Be kind and encouraging with your dear self.

INVITATION

Sometime today, stop. Stop and look at your life from a bird's-eye view. See the good stuff. Name it. Write it. Acknowledge how you are growing. Offer yourself a few encouraging thoughts or words.

More Than Words

We often feel so much more than words can express. Have you noticed how, sometimes, much more can be communicated in silence? It's a worthwhile contemplation. What are the ways we can share this great depth of feeling without words? We can move our bodies to music. We can move our bodies in silence. We can offer our loving gaze. We can offer our full quiet presence. We can touch, letting our heart pour through our hands. We can paint, sculpt, photograph. We can hum. What if there were no words? How would we bridge the distance between ourselves and another? How can we share ourselves fully without relying on verbal exchange? Can we hold ourselves, another, the world, with Cancerian care without making a sound? Can we feel how every gesture we offer into the world can be a vehicle for love?

INVITATION

Today, feel how every gaze can carry compassion or detachment. Experiment today with the world without words. Offer the bounty of yourself without language.

Cancer

Neptune

The Moon and Neptune are both deeply connected to Cancer. Neptune offers dream time, imagination, and extra doses of sensitivity. Neptune fuses, blends, and dissolves us into oneness. Neptune can also rule disillusionment, depression, and addiction. So on a day when we're feeling a lot, we have a Neptune choice. Do we deflate or inspire? It's good to listen to beautiful music on a day like this. It's good to watch a favorite movie. Can there be poetry? If possible, let's spend some time near water, an ocean or a bathtub. Let's also practice melting our more rigid edges. Let's feel the waves of our breath. Let's remember how liquid we actually are. Neptune invites us to slow our breathing, soften our gaze, and imagine ourselves offering up all our worries and wounds to the ocean of compassion, great love, and wisdom. The ocean can remind us that a huge love can always hold us and offer perspective even when we are most raw.

INVITATION

Run water in the tub. Buy a little fountain. Listen to ocean sounds for real or on your phone. Put yourself in water. Let it wash away something you no longer need to carry.

Feeling Words

Today, I'd like us all to create a collage of feeling words. Why? Because when we can specifically name what we are feeling, we can either magnify and grow the feeling or set it free and let it move on and through us. So here is a possible feeling collage: weary, uplifted, sad, stuck, playful, empowered, creative, outraged, lost, unsure. Amazed, kind, passionate, peaceful, anxious, heavy, delighted, joyful, indecisive, determined, focused, annoyed, agitated, loving, gleeful, shocked, resentful, light-hearted, eager, discouraged, tender, fearful, insecure, energetic, bold, artistic, depressed, sexy, powerful, healthy, desperate, exhausted, uncomfortable, excited, refreshed, optimistic. And you?

INVITATION

Write a list of your own words. Be a scribe for your inner life. Surprise yourself, dare yourself, reveal yourself. Tell the truth. Circle the three most potent feeling words. Ask yourself if they are feelings you'd like to magnify or transform. Know that you have the power to do either.

Cancer

Tend to the Tender

Let's tend to the tender within. Let's call upon our own gentler spirits to soothe the weary travelers that we are. This is a dusty, rugged, wild journey we're walking. And some days we need streams of self-forgiveness or a love that listens. This morning, I put my hand on my heart and welcomed the return home. The heart weeps and the hand can heal. The heart says, "I have felt heavy" and the hand says, "let me soothe you." On a day like today, if lists are to be made, let's not list what we haven't yet managed to accomplish. Let's note the ways we are softer, kinder, stronger, more willing. Let's acknowledge the journey—not a moment's imperfection. Let us let ourselves be.

INVITATION

I love Hamlet's two little words near the end of the play. He simply says, "Let be." There is a release, a surrender, an acceptance in those two little words. Try them out today: "Let be."

Mama Love

Cancer is all about maternal love. Today, let's write three beautiful things about our mother or about a positive mom or role model in our life. Or simply write three beautiful things about someone who mothered us. We could even write, "I am the daughter of Rita Marie Trager." Or "I was exquisitely mothered by Mimi Moore." Let's honor the lineage of the feminine today, even if the one who mothered us wasn't female. Let's name three beautiful things or tell a little story about a great nourishing mama love being in our life. Too often, these stories are untold or these qualities are simply taken for granted. Let's honor the big fierce mama love of Cancer today.

INVITATION

It's easier now than ever to document stories. We can interview our parents, our grandparents. We can listen to their stories. Maybe today or in the next weeks, reach out to your mother, an aunt, your grandmother, or any beloved maternal figure and ask if you can celebrate their life through questions and conversation.

Cancer

Revolution of Care

Today, our greatest work is to open our arms wider and continue to expand our definition of family. We are in this together. We have to dare to fall a little more in love with one another. We are as interdependent as we've ever been. This is the moment to nourish one another in all the ways we know how. How far are we willing to extend ourselves beyond our own self-protection? Are we each willing to enlarge our concept of family?

INVITATION

How can you make this more tangible? Choose one person every day outside your usual circle of care. Choose in some way to offer kindness, practical help, understanding, or friendship. Practice inclusion. Let yourself, in some small way, inaugurate a revolution of care. No gesture is too small.

I Belong

Cancer likes to make things whole. It knows how to create a kind of oneness from many parts. It's very inclusive and never wants anything or anyone to be left out. The irony is that sometimes under Cancer, we feel outside the wholeness. This is the paradox and line of growth we hold when we work with the Cancerian energy. We work to wrap our arms around all of it (the feelings, the pain, the growth, the possibility) and we include ourselves in that embrace. We must open to be held even as we hold the wholeness.

INVITATION

Let's use this prompt: "I belong . . ."

Cancer

Welcome to My House

Once upon a time, I traveled to Monterey, California, with a great group of friends to visit another sweet pal who has Cancer rising and was hosting us for the weekend. We parked at the bottom of her drive and began to walk to the house. We suddenly heard music: "Welcome to My House" by Flo Rida. And our friend came dancing down the drive, singing, welcoming us to her home. It was an unforgettable moment. Today, I invite you to play a song that you love and have a dance party invocation, welcoming all kinds of bounty, blessings, and beautiful energy to your house.

INVITATION

Listen to any song today that is about home. Sing along.

Eating Our Troubles

I have a very Cancerian teacher who sometimes says, "I will gladly eat your troubles." She says this because she knows how to digest and assimilate emotional chaos and because she embodies the energy of the protective mother. Cancer rules the stomach. We all need to learn to eat our troubles and not eat *because* we have troubles. We devour *with love*. Cancerian energy can be lovingly fierce!

INVITATION

Read or study a little about Kali and Durga. These gorgeous, powerful Hindu goddesses embody fierce love. Try on a little of that ferocity.

Cancer

Our Cancer Pals

Here are the reasons it's great to have a Cancer friend:

1. They feel you. They feel what you're feeling and they love you through it.

2. They offer mama love. They feed you delicious food. They make sure you have what you need.

3. They often have cozy, warm homes and they are welcoming to guests.

4. They care about humanity as their family, as well as their own little family.

5. They are inclusive.

6. They don't need to say a lot to make you feel better. They can sit next to you or hold your hand or send you a beautiful picture, and you feel their deep love.

7. They are great with children and animals.

8. Their compassion is vast.

9. They can also be amazing producers. They're resourceful and know how to make something happen.

10. They always try to lessen the pain and suffering in the world.

11. They will wrap their arms around you and say, "Grow, grow. I love you."

Hurray, for our beautiful Cancer pals.

INVITATION

Reach out to all your Cancer pals today to tell them how much you love them and why!

Alone

There are times when we are alone when we allow the mask to soften. If we are putting on a good face or somehow pushing through, we finally stop and allow ourselves to be with ourselves. We don't want to be anything or anyone other than we are. We don't want to pretend, impress, offer concern, or manage. We want stillness, silence, and truth. We shed what is not necessary. We beckon what soothes. Sometimes we dare to be in that rare, raw, unmasked state with one another. This is not simply being free with our emotional state, without filtering. This is a conscious choice to be present and flowing with one another, without hiding. This takes practice and willingness and even curiosity.

INVITATION

Do a little energetic scan of your face, jaw, scalp, brow, eyes. If you are holding any tension, choose to release it. It is easier to do this when alone. But practice being deeply surrendered with others you trust. Practice being with others without the need to constantly respond.

Cancer

Nothing to Fix

I'll be honest. I often look around our house and make a list of all its imperfections. I have twenty ways I want to fix, remodel, and redo our house. And certainly home improvements feel great, but sometimes it's good to look around and say, "This is our home. This is our shelter. This is our hearth. I will trust that, as I change and grow, my home will organically and beautifully reflect that. There is no rush. There is no lack today. I will see only the beauty of a space we are blessed to inhabit. Today, I will feel that the walls, mirrors, art, furniture, floors, kitchen, pots, and windows all reflect back the love of we who live within. There's nothing to fix today. Today, I will feel and know my heart and hearth and home to be as one."

INVITATION

Today, celebrate what is working. Save "fixing" for another day. Take the time to notice all that is supporting you at the moment, all that is working in your favor. Allow your body to feel and know that all will be attended to in the right timing.

Prose Poem

If today were a prose poem, it might sound something like this: "She was sad, curled in on herself, unable to find the right words. Those words might free her from the numbness that gathered around her face and throat. The feelings were big and leaked out though she tried to manage and contain them, but they were messy and lumpy and uncooperative. She stumbled her way outside and sat in the sun. *Ah, yes, that's the warmth of the sun on my face and it feels good.* She could name that. She sat outside a long while and let nature whisper open all the closed places inside her. She felt the mother of the world rock her with her breeze and awe her with so many butterflies. She listened outside herself, and that felt good. Finally, as the sun began to set, she felt something warm at the center of her chest. It was growing. She knew she had to move her body. She needed music, music that would move her someplace new. She stood up and felt something like relief, something like release, a homecoming, a coming home to herself."

INVITATION

Write your own prose poem. Use the third person to explore your life with a slight distance. Read it to someone you trust.

Cancer

Quiver and Bless

Cancer always offers two options. The crab walks sideways, armored, protecting itself from pain and securing its home front, or it reaches for the sun, exposes it soft underbelly, quivers, and offers its love. At a time when every day we receive painful news of the world and every day we navigate our own personal pain and struggles, Cancer invites us to stay open, to keep our eyes and our hearts open. We will quiver in the vulnerability and heart-ache, but we will grow. We stay present and open so we can, in whatever small way, offer our love to those in pain. We quiver and bless. We try not to hide, numb out, or get jaded. Cancer asks us to feel the wholeness of humanity and love and bless this huge family.

INVITATION

Work with this idea: If there is fear, then quiver. But always follow it with an offering: Don't allow fear to win. Quivering is the first step to releasing the fear and moving toward blessing.

Grunkly

Some days we wake up feeling *grunkly* (yes, I made that up), also known as *feeling the feels*. Let's call this day: Name the Feeling Day. When we name something, we can either diffuse its power or actually strengthen that feeling for the good. For example, some days we wake up feeling wretched, but our job is to find out the ingredients of the wretchedness. We might feel a little sad because we wish we had more time for ourselves. We might feel irritated because our back hurts. We might feel restless because our schedule has been demanding. We always feel better writing about it, seeing it on the page, or speaking about it—and then inviting in a little self-forgiveness, tenderness, and inspiration. Yes, let's name the wretchedness and then take time to breathe in replenishment.

INVITATION

Make up your own word for feeling wretched. Have fun with it. Say it with zeal and enthusiasm. Teach it to someone. Let it diffuse some of the pain.

Cancer

Mother of the World

I recently heard a story of a woman who attended a retreat, and at the end of the event, the leader asked everyone to be "a mother to the world"—to offer mother love to this planet. He asked everyone regardless of gender, and everyone felt the potency of his request. What does it mean to mother the world? We need to feed and clothe all. We need to nourish and educate all. We need to hold all in love. We need everyone to have a home. We offer tenderness and practicality. We offer encouragement and strength. We work to be harmless with the earth itself. We work to be harmless with one another. We hold those in pain. We tend to those suffering. We find a way to meet and fix any present problem. We care for the entire human family.

INVITATION

Start within and work outward. Nourish your tender self, nourish your immediate family, and then open even wider. Mother the world by extending your circle of care with tiny loving acts.

Feel and Express

As we stand at the threshold between Cancer and Leo, we can ask how they work together. Cancer says, "I'm feeling everything today." And Leo says, "Let's create something with all that feeling." Cancer says, "I'd like to stay home tonight and be cozy." And Leo says, "Then I'll bring the party to you. See you at six." Cancer will always lend its emotional sensitivity, creative intelligence, and resourcefulness to whatever Leo creates and Leo will always lend its courage and confidence to Cancer's compassion. Today, don't hide what you feel. Dare to express what might feel like too much. Let the feeling simply be fuel for your next gesture toward the light. Today, let your tender, full heart create.

INVITATION

As we ready ourselves for Leo, call a friend and plan a date! See a play! Go to an art gallery. Welcome Leo with an appreciation for art and beauty! And fun!

Leo

Welcoming Leo

Today, we welcome Leo! Leo is the great sign of identity, leadership, and courage. It rules the heart and leads from the heart,
kindling the hearts of others. "To encourage" actually comes
from the French word *coeur*, for "heart." Under Leo, we have the
opportunity to grow the flames of our own heart and act with
generosity and authenticity. We come forth as our full, expressive
selves, and that alone can inspire and encourage others. Leo
offers warmth and reminds us that a little love goes a long way.
Under Leo, we let our heart and not our to-do list lead the way.

INVITATION

Place your left hand on your heart and your right hand on your belly.
Remember Cancer rules the stomach and Leo rules the heart. Feel
the shift of signs in your body. Let your attention move from the
stomach to the fiery center or your being—your heart. Breathe.

Leo

360 Degrees

Let's do a little experiment. Let's ask ourselves what one quality we'd like to embody more. What is something in ourselves we'd like to magnify? Courage, peace, confidence? Let's close our eyes and place that word at the center of our Leo heart and send that quality out like the sun's rays, 360 degrees. We can breathe deeply to extend the quality. We can feel our heart as the center of the sun and let the heat of the heart magnify what we wish to grow within ourselves. Let's return again and again to this practice. Embodiment facilitates change.

INVITATION

Start with a blank sheet of paper and begin to brainstorm. List a bunch of qualities you'd like to magnify or embody. Don't edit or critique. Spend 10 to 15 minutes just generating ideas. Then, circle one or two that truly stand out and start to work with those words. If you'd like to use a little Leo artistry, choose one of the words, draw or paint a sun, and place that word at the center! Hang it somewhere where you will see it daily.

Leadership

Presidents, kings, and queens are all in the Leo lineage. Leo is a great sign of leadership, and the best leaders embody the energy of the conscious and loving Leo. A conscious and loving leader's self-interests are eclipsed by the needs, cries, and voices of the people. A true and conscious Leo leader stands for the *we* and never the singular *I*. A true and conscious leader facilitates and does not dictate, is generous, and willingly shines the light on all in her orbit. And a true and conscious leader offers wisdom—the marriage of intelligence and love. May we all stand, each and all, as Leo leaders in our own lives and welcome new leaders who will lead with love and conscience.

INVITATION

It's always an interesting exercise to ask ourselves what leadership styles we admire. Who do you feel is standing in their power in a way that inspires you? Today, if you have time, read about a leader who has touched you in some way. Ask yourself if there is a quality in their leadership that you'd like to cultivate.

Leo

Our Child Self

Leo rules our spontaneous, child self. It rules unobstructed radiance and inspires us to authentically dive into the world again and again. Today, remember the hope and possibility of being ten years old. Let your child self whisper their dreams in your ear. Let your innocence offer a willingness to see life afresh. Leo says, "Let's play. Let's offer our superpowers. Let's get on our bikes and ride. Let's taste and celebrate moments of joy and let them carry us through our darker hours."

INVITATION

Write about a day from your childhood that you remember well or write about a gift you were given as a child that made your heart sing.

Hello, Love

My daughter used to say "I-You" instead of "I love you." She skipped the word *love* but ended up saying something that reveals the greater truth. I-You. When we love, we know the other as a mirrored self. We understand the paradox. We are each unique and individual and also can begin to see and know our oneness with another. Under Leo, we move from the desire to be the one and only spotlighted self to the generous, inclusive self. *Me* becomes *we* and *we* becomes *one*. Leo knows its own radiance and greets the radiance in everyone she meets. Our individual radiance becomes collective radiance. Our individual love becomes one vast, unceasing love. I-You.

INVITATION

Try this practice today. It's what I call the "Hello, Love" experiment. You might feel shy at first but allow yourself to keep practicing. It's a subtle, potent, beautiful exchange. And yes, you can definitely start by just "thinking it"!

Meet someone's eyes.

Think (or say): "Hello, love."

See what happens.

Risk and repeat.

Leo

Leave Beauty in Your Wake

Today, I wish for us all the deep understanding that we, every day, can leave beauty in our wake. I wish for us to know that we can repeatedly summon courage to show up in the world anew and in our courage, make each day more beautiful. Leo rules courage; and Leo encourages us to fail and flail while we are learning, while we are becoming. Let us infuse today with the strength and magnificence of our courageous hearts, the hearts that give us strength to step forward in the name of beauty. May the light of our hearts, the light we are, shine through our stubborn closures. May we each be a courageous light in the world, leaving beauty in our wake through each authentic word and gesture.

INVITATION

Today, imagine that wherever you walk or travel, you leave a river of light in your wake. Imagine even that your gestures or glances leave light in their wake. Let's be conscious of what we leave behind, what we offer to the world through our movement in it. Walk down the street and imagine you are lighting up the path for those who follow.

Fall in Love

Fall in love with someone. Yes, you've heard correctly. Fall in love! When our heart is open and courageous and willing, we can create beauty in any relationship we choose. We can fall into love with anyone and celebrate that waterfall of goodness. Let's fall in love with the mailman, the little kid on the subway who looks a little blue, our cranky boss. We can find the beauty in every living thing and choose to grow that beauty into gratitude, appreciation, celebration, love. Choose to be in love. Walk in love. Fall in love whenever possible today.

INVITATION

You have your marching orders! Go forth and fall in love. The trees and flowers and buildings and vendors and your very self are all waiting for you to fall in love this very minute.

Leo

Receive the Sun

I'd like us to remember how it feels when we step outside on a perfect day and the sun touches our skin in such a way that we want to stop, turn up our face, and open our body to that generous warmth. We feel how the warmth seeps beneath the surface and somehow softens us inside and out. We grow quiet and grateful for this endless source of heat and light and sustenance. Our life practice is to receive love as we receive the sun. And, yes, to give love as the sun, which effortlessly shines on all, warms all, touches all. It's like breathing—warmth in, warmth out, light in, light out, love in, love out.

INVITATION

Leo reminds us that as long as the sun shines, we can grow beneath it. Our child selves are nourished. We can be like bold sunflowers with strong spines and expansive blooms. Some time today, stand in the sun—if there is sun—and turn your face up toward its warmth. Feel the light on your face. Feel the light like the love of the kindest parent. Know that light is the texture of love. And say yes.

Love Looks Like You

Calling all superheroes! Calling all of us—every last one of us. Courage, fortitude, and love required. If fires are raging, it's time to burn away any last bit of not enough, I don't know how, or who me? It's time to summon our inner reserves of hope and vigilance, tenacity and compassion. Sometimes that looks like being very still and sending copious amounts of love to a struggling humanity. Sometimes that looks like firefighters on the front lines. Sometimes hope, vigilance, tenacity, courage, compassion, love looks like *you* right now, breathing, steadying yourself, and leaning into the light.

INVITATION

What if *love* looked exactly like *you* right now, even in all your imperfections? What if *courage* looked exactly like *you* right now, in all your imperfections? What if we could all embrace the fact that we have a unique gift to give and today is the day to give it? Try to offer yourself in some small but potent way today. You are needed!

Leo

Courage

Where do you require the most courage in your life right now? Is there something that needs to be said? Do you require courage to change a pattern of behavior? Do you need to take your work game to another level? Do you need better boundaries in some area? Is there a big ask you've been putting off? Does some big love need to be expressed? When we are in Leo, we are not meant to hide in any way. We summon all kinds of courage to authentically show up in our lives in new ways. We summon the fire to express. We call upon the power and passion of the Leo heart to lead the way.

INVITATION

Encouragement and courage are deeply connected. When we feel encouraged, we dare to take courageous steps. We have to kindle the fires of our heart with love and inspiration, so we dare ourselves into our next unfolding. Today, ask for encouragement or offer it to yourself. Take a tiny, courageous step forward.

Our Leo Friends

Here are the reasons it's great to have a Leo friend:

1. They're a party unto themselves. They bring light and presence to any event.

2. They are generous and loving. Leo rules the heart, after all.

3. They're dramatic and theatrical and make life interesting.

4. They are courageous. They know how to roar when a roar is needed.

5. They also know how to nap when a nap is needed.

6. They encourage you to express yourself fully. They are fully themselves and they want you to be the same.

7. They love to play and be spontaneous.

8. They love to create. Give them a paintbrush or food or some clay or a guitar, and they will find a way to work with the medium and say, "this is me."

9. They don't mind taking charge or leading the way.

10. The sun rules Leo. So your Leo pal is pretty bright and radiant.

11. They will beam their sunshine selves on you, full of appreciation and love.

Yay for our Leo pals.

INVITATION

Reach out to your Leo friends to tell them how much you love them and why!

Welcoming

We are forever either welcoming others into our lives or closing the door and staying safe. Welcoming requires openness. It requires an invitation. It requires a generosity of spirit. Every day, we have the opportunity to welcome the day, welcome our colleagues, warmly welcome our friends and loved ones. We even have the opportunity to welcome someone with whom we may disagree to converse in an open way. Of course, there are times when we need solitude, when we need to welcome quiet and our own good company. But so often we close the door or close our hearts out of fear or shyness or habit. Who and/or what might we welcome today? How can we show our welcome? How can we simply, genuinely extend our warmth? We all need welcoming on a daily basis. We can welcome and open to receive welcoming.

INVITATION

A welcoming spirit is reflected in our bodies. It is offered through a warm gaze, a soft jaw, an open torso. It is even communicated in the depth of our breath. Today, as you walk through your day, notice your own body and whether it feels welcoming.

Purr

Stretch, purr, roar, hunt, nap. Let's make that deliciousness the plan for the day. One of the most direct routes to joy is to get the body moving, to feel ourselves dancing with all that is. So stretch and dance and run and skip then purr. And by that, I mean, let's ease into the day by touching base with what feels nourishing, by remembering and interacting with what we love. Then roar, let's roar our gifts, our passions, our love into the world. And how about hunt? Leo gives us the courage to pursue what we are after. It is powerful. Leo leads the pursuit. It works hard for an intense, short, potent burst. And then yes, you guessed it, naps. Every good day has a rest built in, a full-bodied complete surrender. Leo insists on feline fun, and that always includes a nap.

INVITATION

Even if you are not a "nap person," lie down for 5 minutes today and completely surrender. Let all the stress and busyness be absorbed by the earth beneath you. Completely let go. See how even five minutes can be a glorious reset.

Leo

The Heart

Leo rules the generous heart, the courageous heart, the bold heart, and the broken heart. It rules the beating heart, the blazing heart, the universal heart, and the fiery heart. Leo rules the heart of the matter, the heart of the story, the heart that is home. Leo rules your heart and my heart and the one great heart.

INVITATION

How does your heart feel today? What is the quality that is shining through? Write about it for 10 minutes.

What to Do with Sadness

Here are two stanzas from my poem, "What to Do with Sadness":

When sadness lingers,
When loneliness creeps in to sit beside you
And will not leave,
When you can no longer feel a spark of joy
In even a hidden corner,

Find something,
Anything
That is burning —
A star,
A porch lamp,
A candle on the table.

INVITATION

We look to the light to help us out of our closures. Today, find a light—a candle, the fire of your heart, or the sun. Then open to it. Pull your shoulders back and feel the front surface of your heart. Take a deep breath. Let the sadness begin to dissolve in the light.

Leo

You Are a Poem

Here is a poem I wrote. Read it slowly and out loud:

*You
Are a poem.
Your birth,
A captured moment
Of the mystery.
Your intricate design,
A gift of planets
Dancing.*

*You
Are a poem.
Each part of you
Specifically chosen
To be read aloud,
Into the world,
Born to unfurl
Your vibrant freedom.*

*A map of the heavens
Illumined through your song,
Your invitation,
Ever and always,
To follow that map,
Walk in love,
Live the poetry
You are.*

INVITATION

Read this poem out loud to a friend. Call them up or knock on their door. Offer it as a gift.

Play

Play if you can. Play even if you are at work. I have a friend who used to be in charge of a big communications team. And every Wednesday they had "Weird Food Wednesday." Whenever any member of the team traveled, they would bring back something unusual or hilarious to eat and they would all try it on Wednesday. Let's see what we can do to take it easy or be more spontaneous or lighthearted today. It's so important to find moments to simply welcome a little more ease, a little less pressure. Let's ask ourselves today one simple question: How can we lighten up?

INVITATION

Today, tell me about what makes you feel most playful and light-hearted. Let's use this writing prompt: "I feel most light when I . . ."

Leo

The Sun Inside

Some days the sun is nowhere to be seen. Gray days can be lovely and true and reflective. We need the quiet invitation of a gray day. Leo, however, would offer this: Always learn to locate the sun inside. That doesn't mean always be cheery and bright. And that doesn't mean we have to scramble to be optimistic all the time. It simply means that, even on an inner or outer gray day, Leo's gift is to remind us that our fiery heart is beating quite apart from anything we are feeling. Our body is warm and alive and experiencing the day because our Leo sun heart is doing its work.

INVITATION

Take a moment, close your eyes, and feel your heart. Then, begin to feel outward with the energy of the heart. Don't blaze outward, just let the warmth and light of the heart make its way as far as you can imagine from your center. Let the light—that tender, curious light—be like the first streams of dawn illuminating everything it touches. And when you are ready, return to the home you are, the house of the rising sun.

A Pride of Humans

We can wake with a languid lion stretch and a gigantic yawn. We can slowly survey our day and decide when and how we want to move out into it. No rushing allowed. We might even need a glorious catnap in the sun—the ultimate Leo treat. Did I mention a nap so close to waking? I did. We could pounce and play and express our fine, feline, fabulous selves. Let's own our majesty and sovereignty. It's OK. We are all beautiful radiant lights unto ourselves, bright and strong. Of course, when we gather as a group, the light and majesty grows; a pride of lions is a sight to behold. What if we gathered as a pride of humans? I don't mean that we need to be full of ourselves, but that together we can be even more filled with our soul selves and radiate that outward.

INVITATION

I invite you to look out and around the next crowd you find yourself in and dare to call the gathering a "pride of humans." Something about that phrase calls us to a higher expression of ourselves. What if we looked out at our fellow humans and saw them as capable of giving more, capable of loving more. What if we named them something that inspired us all to take a step up!

Leo

Gloriously Imperfect

Leo asks us all to be generous with ourselves. Leo says, "Yes, we are all gloriously imperfect, but let's share who we are. We can't let fear or self-criticism win the day." Leo says, "Express, express, express. Don't compromise your light. It takes courage to offer our true selves in the world. What are we waiting for?" Leo says, "There's precisely one of each of us and thus we are all deeply necessary in this crazy grand puzzle of life. We can't let ourselves get lost under the rug. Leo says, "Sparkle, shine, quietly glow, but offer yourself—shy or bold, offer your gifts, offer your love." Leo also reminds us to be sure to appreciate and love all those other radiant selves shining forth. No one light is more significant than another. We all must light the way. Leo says this is going to be fun.

INVITATION

If ever you feel shy, think about generosity. Sometimes if we reframe a situation and think of speaking up as a *gift* to the group, it's easier to offer ourselves. Think about how you might be generous with yourself today. So many people benefit when we dare to share our light.

Jaguar

A woman once told me this story: She was in South America on an adventure tour of sorts in one of the tropical rainforests. She was in a tent and, in the middle of the afternoon while she was taking a nap, a jaguar walked into her tent and lay down next to her. She knew she couldn't scream and she knew she shouldn't move. Apparently, this was a big female Jaguar. So, she lay there with a jaguar and tried to be as calm as she could. She matched the breathing of the jaguar. She breathed in her strength. She did not move. Instead, she simply let go. Three hours later, the jaguar stood up, looked at her, and left. The woman learned something about presence and courage that day. She carried the spirit of the jaguar—its power, strength, and grace—into her forever changed life.

INVITATION

Close your eyes and imagine this exact scenario. Put yourself in that tent and imagine the jaguar. Imagine that she lays her huge body right next to yours. And then breathe. Breathe in your sovereignty and her majesty. Breathe in her sheer power. How do you feel? How does your body feel?

Leo

Turning Ten

Do you remember your tenth birthday? Two digits! Do you remember that moment? It felt like adulthood. We held up both hands to show our age and felt deliriously excited about what was to come. Leo rules our child sunshine self. It rules unobstructed radiance. It rules the daring it takes to offer the authentic self to the world again and again. Today, remember the hope and possibility and major threshold of ten. Let your child self whisper her dreams in your ear. Let your innocence offer willingness to see life afresh.

INVITATION

Let's write. Put a big number *10* at the top of the page and dive in. What do you remember? What does your child self have to say to you today? What would your child self whisper in your ear?

Blaze and Rest

Leo asks us to be as the sun. And what does the sun do? It rises each day—rhythmically, consistently, graciously. It shines its light and offers its light to all, without discrimination, without hesitation. It illuminates the dark. The sun is a great symbol of generosity. It grows what it touches. It keeps us alive. It offers vitality. I like to think about "the heart of the sun"—the molten lava love core, the soul of the sun. When we each act as the sun, we cannot help but shine as love, melting all separation and barriers that stand in the way of a loving relationship. When in Leo, we all have the opportunity to offer our warmth and light for the benefit of all. But what else does the sun do? We all experience its setting. It does not blaze indefinitely on one area. It rests. We experience its offering cyclically. So, too, can we blaze and rest. Have a gorgeous, warm radiant day.

INVITATION

Let's work with this sentence: "The sun grows what it touches." If we are the sun, let's think today of everything we touch and how our touch can facilitate growth. This is a day to notice how and what you touch and the light and love you communicate in that touch.

Leo

If We Choose

If all who read this today choose at this very moment to take a deeper breath than usual and then another, and then place a hand on their heart and take another breath, we effect change. If we choose at this moment to offer our yearning, crinkly, imperfect self a dose of love, if we even say out loud, "I love you," we effect change. And if we then hold someone in our heart that needs our love in this moment, if again, we say out loud, "I love you," we effect change. And if we stay quiet for a moment breathing love, then my friends, the world grows lighter, as do we. Will you join me?

INVITATION

If you will, place your hand on your heart and breathe. Then, read what is written above out loud. Read slowly enough that the invitation can sink in.

Brave and Kind

Leo asks us to be brave and to be kind. Leo asks us to express ourselves fully but not for fame or adulation. It asks us to express ourselves so we might inspire or uplift or encourage. It asks us to shine so we might remind others of their light. Leo likes to be in charge; but the first step to being a truly beneficent ruler is to listen. Leo asks us to check our ego at the door and walk across the threshold as one who is interested in the gifts of others. It asks us to be courageously loving with one another. It asks us to think with our heart and love with our mind.

INVITATION

Today, ask questions all day. Check in with others. Hear their stories. Encourage them to share. Listen. Be deeply interested in the gifts of others.

Leo

Best Selves

Think festive, frolicsome. Think playful, light. Think party. Think childlike wonder, spontaneity, candles burning bright, belly laughter. Think loud and joyous. Think board games, charades, movie sprees. Think love. Leo offers the opportunity to share our best selves. Leo says, "Show up and roar your soul self into the room, or purr your soul self into a space." Leo says, "Don't hide. Be who you are. Don't apologize. Own it." Leo celebrates how unique we each are. Oh, it's a good day! Friends, grow the light, fan the flames, grow your heart fire. Be generous with yourself. Let your love pour forth for all who are thirsty.

INVITATION

Get dressed up today for no reason at all. Or create a reason. Throw a spontaneous party and tell your guest "we're getting all dressed up and fabulous because we can!"

The Love That Never Ceases

Today, let the sun and everything it stands for fill the day. The sun rules Leo. Let the warmth, the heat, and the light of the sun prevail. Let the sun, which is the heart at the center of your chest, radiate its goodness. Breathe in warmth and exhale your most sensitive, generous self. Let love melt inner struggle. Let love soften outer struggle. Let love fall upon you like a balm. Let love envelop you. There's a love that never ceases and it pervades everything and everyone. And we are the conduits for that love. Today, let's be grateful that we are capable of palpably, tangibly, completely loving another and lifting another with that love. Today, let us offer gratitude, love, and our kindled hearts.

INVITATION

Here is your writing prompt: "The love that never ceases."

Leo

One Branch

Here's a little Leo story. There is a tree in our neighborhood that I see daily. Actually, it's one branch that speaks to me. There's a big branch that reaches far out in its usual direction and then, suddenly, completely stops short and shoots straight upward. It's the only branch upright and reaching to the sky. I always think two things: (1) Wow, that branch was not going to be stopped. It ran into obstruction and completely changed its course. And (2) How brave and strong, clear and daring that branch looks. It emanates: "I will always find a way." In short, that branch can offer a lot about how to live our lives.

INVITATION

Is there something in your life that requires you to stand upright and switch course right now? How can you be daring and determined as you do so?

Cheering On the Light

Let's talk a bit about comparison. How many of us get caught
in the ongoing struggle of "I'm not as bright, light, rich, pretty,
handsome, talented, tall, thin, brilliant as . . ." How many of us cast
ourselves as behind, not enough, less interesting than? It's tricky
territory. The fact is, we are all here to grow our light and to share
more of the inherent love we are. That's Leo in action. But we get
caught in the comparison and jealousy dance. Here's the deal.
We are each a sun self. How can we compare suns? It's futile. We
can praise suns and honor suns and be grateful for suns. We can
practice remembering that one sun self does not reduce or mini-
mize another. My sun self can never eclipse yours. Can we practice
cheering on the light, wherever and in whomever we see it?

INVITATION

Practice noticing when you feel jealous. Take note that you may be
jealous of something you could actually work on growing in your
own life. And meanwhile, do your best to offer love and admiration
to all who inspire you. There is room for all.

Leo

Leo Directives

Here are some beautiful Leo directives written by my astrologer father, Michael David Robbins:

1. Accept and promote all other selves.

2. Assure others—what you are is good.

3. Be the loving heart of those you gather around.

4. Call humanity's attention to the source of light within each being.

5. Walk the earth as a radiant sun of love and wisdom.

INVITATION

Today, let's all work on the first directive! Whom might we promote today? Whom might we uplift and assure today?

Thaw

Once, when I traveled to Finland in the late winter, I looked to the ice beneath my feet. It was clear that the ground had frozen and thawed many times in the previous months. The ice was thick but seemed to have layers. There were many days it felt very gray. But there were particular moments when the sun emerged that the landscape became vibrantly alive. The sun reflected off the white snow and became a dance of endless light. Sometimes we all feel like that snow that has frozen to ice and been thawed multiple times. The thawing is the practice. The melting is a way of life. It is almost impossible to deny the sun—in the sky and in our hearts. And yet, we all sometimes manage to stay closed and iced for too long. Leo invites us to return again and again to embody and share the warmth of the sun—to receive the rays of the heart.

INVITATION

Go outside today. Close your eyes and turn your face to the sun. Imagine the front surface of your body thawing, melting, and softening. Breathe deeply and let it soften even more. Soak in the warmth and generosity of the sun.

Leo

One Last Hurrah

This is the threshold time between Leo and Virgo. I always like to say that Leo throws the party and Virgo cleans it up. Our fiery expression is soon going to be packaged and produced in lovingly efficient ways. We are moving out of the expansion of Leo into the meticulous care and practical work of Virgo. Is there any last Leo gesture you want to make?

INVITATION

Throw yourself a final Leo party before we welcome Virgo! You might take yourself out to dinner or give yourself a full night off from work or worry.

Virgo

Welcoming Virgo

Virgo carries great devotion. She uses that devotion to improve and perfect the material world or physical form so it can be a conduit for beauty and love. Virgo is willing to scrub, root out, cleanse, clean up, or purify a space, an idea, or a piece of art so that it reflects and holds an energy that is refined and true. Virgo has the ultimate editorial eye. There is an art to refinement, and this is Virgo's domain. Virgo knows how to make it just right before sending the creation out into the world. It does not skip a single step. It will not release her project until it has been worked over, adjusted, perfected, and streamlined. During the Virgo season, we can ask ourselves where the industrious, purifying energy of Virgo will benefit us the most. Do we want to focus on our physical health? Do we want to devote ourselves to a certain emotional, mental, or spiritual practice? Do we want to wrap up a project with a keen eye and measured hand? The earthy energy of Virgo will get it done and get it done well.

INVITATION

Today, spend some time thinking about an area of your life that would benefit from Virgo's refining energy. Will this be a month of health and well-being? Or a month of editing and perfecting? Open the door to wellness today.

Good Work

Most of us desire to do good work in the world—work that is true to who we are and work that improves our lives and the lives of others. Virgo is the sign that rules hard work and our truest service. Whenever Virgo is strongly present, there is an inner impulse to get to it, apply oneself, waste not another moment. But, often simultaneously, we can feel inadequate or imperfect, not up for our true work. Somehow Virgo turns up the volume on our most insistent, inner, critical voices. "What's the use? It will never be enough. Others have and will do it better." We talk ourselves out of the work we'd love to do before we have fully given ourselves to it. Let's try a gentler way. Let's meet our inner critic with compassion and an uncommon will. Perhaps we say, "And still I will press forward." Or, "And still, I must give myself wholeheartedly to this." We try to remember that our love for the work that's right for us will dissuade our insufficiencies. We must, in a way, be practical and grounded to proceed with our devotion. How do we move forward clearly and deliberately? What is the next step on our journey toward the work we love? Let's continue to progress. Virgo invites us to lovingly apply ourselves.

INVITATION

Let's write: My good work is . . .

Simplicity

Today is the perfect day to grow a little quieter and listen for the inner shifts we can each make to feel healthier. The month of Virgo invites us to streamline our lives, attend to our sleep, our food, our work patterns. How can we live more simply? How can we spend more time, love, and energy on the things that matter most to us? Be as silent as you can today. Imagine we are all preparing to tend to our bodies and spirits with a deeper level of care. Virgo asks us to refine and purify, to clarify and eliminate. It asks us to be discerning and it asks us to explore our devotion. What can we love fully and serve well? To what or whom can we offer the bounty of our heart and the excellence of our work? How does discernment feel in our body? How does devotion? Let's breathe them in.

INVITATION

Make a list: Write a few tiny, tiny adjustments that will improve your wellness. These cannot be punitive. They are invitations to shift something slightly that will let more grace flow.

Sprinkled with the Sacred

Yes, Virgo is practical, dutiful, healthy, and smart, but she is also magic. In what way? Virgo understands a lot about connecting with the divine, creating sacred space, about paying exquisite attention to the present and noticing what most do not. Virgo transforms the mundane to the magical. Today, that's available to all of us. What little magical things do you have in store today? What routine tasks could be sprinkled with the sacred? It's almost like a secret we can each carry. We know we're leaving magic in our wake.

INVITATION

The quality of our attention can turn the most mundane task into the most sacred. Today, while washing the dishes or walking the dog, stay fully present and notice what you may not have noticed yesterday. Invite every sense to pay attention. Receive the gifts of an ordinary moment.

Virgo

Daily Doses of Wellness

Here are a few lovely Virgo adjustments or suggestions to bring daily doses of wellness into our day:

1. Walk around the block.
2. Call a dear friend.
3. Take supplements.
4. Refuse to listen to the inner critic.
5. Sit still for 5 minutes.
6. Write.
7. Stretch for 5 minutes.
8. Learn something new.
9. Sing.
10. Get a little extra sleep.
11. Buy flowers.
12. Take a dance break.
13. Plant something.
14. Drink more water.
15. Say a kind word or two to our sweet selves.

INVITATION

Choose one or two of these for the day. Once you've completed them, be sure to celebrate. Don't just say, "Oh, that's nothing." It's something, and it makes a difference in the beauty and bounty of your day.

Mary Poppins

Mary Poppins is a great example of the Virgo-Pisces polarity. As the song says, she is "practically perfect" in every way. She is proper, orderly, and devoted to those in her care, which is very Virgo. But she's also always inviting everyone into the realm of the imagination ruled by Pisces, Virgo's opposite sign. She is both practical Virgo, and whimsical Pisces. Julie Andrews, who originated the role in film, has Virgo rising. She was *perfectly* cast. So let's take a note from Mary today. We can embrace the practicality of Virgo but refuse to lose the poetry of Pisces. We can be precise and playful. We can work hard but leave time for pockets of daydreaming. All work and no play leaves us all a bit dreary. So, let's be sure to find our particular "spoonful of sugar" to keep the day light and our spirits lighter.

INVITATION

Watch Julie Andrews in *Mary Poppins*. And if you love astrology, have a little peek at her astrological chart! What do you notice?

Virgo

Enough

Virgo often likes to whisper two little words: "Not enough." These two little words creep into how we talk to ourselves. I'm not smart enough. I'm not healthy enough. I'm not achieving enough. It's a monologue of self-criticism hard to arrest. Let's turn this around. There's a Buddhist proverb that goes, "Enough is a feast." Yes, enough is a feast. It's enough. We are each enough. We are growing and changing and learning and failing and daring. And it is enough. So, I say enough is enough with not enough.

INVITATION

Do the "enough" dance. Yes, actually get up and dance. Turn up the volume and dance the dance of enough and more than enough. Claim enough for yourself.

Practice

I've been thinking about the saying, "Practice makes perfect." But I believe that perfection is definitely overrated. Trying to be perfect drives us all a little crazy. How about practice makes peace? That is, if we show up in our lives and are willing to practice in the areas where we feel most vulnerable, we will feel increasingly peaceful. Practice is a beautiful thing. We return to something within ourselves that we are trying to strengthen, or we show up again and again to work through tender places. We can also practice our artistry in the world, bringing increasing peace through the beauty offered. I'll sacrifice perfection for greater inner peace any day. Practice makes peace is the perfect blend of Virgo and Pisces. We work on and refine our lives and our contribution to allow for greater love and grace to flow.

INVITATION

The art of practicing is just that—an art. It's a beautiful thing to show up rhythmically for something. And it takes talent and dedication to show up rhythmically. Is there something you would like to practice in your life? Start by showing up for it.

Virgo

An Ocean Awaits

Virgo is a sign of hard work and perfectionism, but it is also deeply related and deeply influenced by its opposite sign, Pisces. Pisces whispers to Virgo that she must remember why she's doing what she is doing. Though there is always work to be done, there is also always an ocean, a beach, music, poetry, and self-compassion. When Virgo is in balance, she begins to listen to Pisces. She quiets the worry or the need to clean her desk again. She walks outside to feel something beyond the list of what is broken or needs to be fixed. She remembers why she works so hard. She wants her world to be ready for love and grace to enter. But when she is in balance, she realizes she will never feel completely ready. And her only course of action is to stop, breathe, and enjoy the bounty and beauty of this world, to feel the joy of stillness and rest.

INVITATION

Today, fix nothing. Today, set worry aside. Today, for at least 10 minutes, invite in the flow and stroll and ease of Pisces. You may rest. You may take a walk. You may eat something nourishing. Today, invite ease.

Tiny Victories

This is a day of renewed devotion and powerful action. We commit to a greater sense of well-being by paying attention to the small stuff. We take a breath or stretch. We light a candle. We choose kind words within. We notice how any given gesture, word, or choice can move us toward greater freedom or greater love. We promise to notice our tiny victories and not dismiss the subtle shifts that relieve pressure or heaviness. We tell a story of progress instead of obstruction. We return again and again to the life choices we know will set us right and we devote ourselves to feeling good as we walk with a lighter step and a wider heart.

INVITATION

This is a day of focusing on tiny tweaks that could make a big difference. Perhaps you could take a walk this morning, once around the block slowly, before you do any work. What other small changes could you make today?

Virgo

Kind To-Dos

Here is a kind Virgo to-do list that I'd love to tackle. Join me?

1. Stop. Breathe. Listen outward to the far edges.
2. Put your hand on your heart and breathe again.
3. Whisper something kind to yourself.
4. Move slowly from A to B.
5. Water a plant.
6. Choose to make one tiny area of the house look beautiful.
7. Drink tea or coffee or whatever is yummy.
8. Sit on the couch for 5 minutes doing nothing.
9. Write a little loving note to someone who could use it. This might include yourself.
10. Breathe some more—slowly, deeply.

INVITATION

Here is a little writing prompt: "What *is* working right now?" Make a list. Start with the beating of your heart.

Remember Why

Sometimes in Virgo, we get too concerned with the perfection of the material world and we drive ourselves and everyone else crazy. We have to remember why we are cleaning or organizing or systematizing. We have to remember why we are purifying or refining or critiquing. Hopefully it's in the name of love or beauty or peace, something that will improve the quality of our living. We also have to ask ourselves *how* we are cleaning or perfecting. That is, are we angry or self-loathing or depressed? Virgo asks us to refine our worlds with compassion, beauty, and sensitivity. At its best, it asks that kindness, care, and critique come together to improve our lives.

INVITATION

Find a moment today to notice and amplify any tiny fraction of joy. Mark it with breath. Or a smile. Or an inner *aha*. Stop or slow down enough to notice, "This is lovely."

Attend

In the name of wellness, let's start at the top of our head and work down. Let's attend to each part of our body. Does it need support or help? If we start at the top, we can call an optometrist or a dentist. Then, if need be, we can address the skin on our face and call a dermatologist. From there, we can see what part of the body we run into next. We can throw in a manicure at some point. Maybe when we get halfway through, we'll book a massage. Also, it will be fun to try to attend to areas we usually ignore. What luscious cream might we put on our elbows? So let's make a body to-do list, but it's also a step-by-step "celebrate this body" list.

INVITATION

Today, right now, call to make an appointment. Delay no longer. Then, put another name in your calendar to call tomorrow. This is a clear and direct action to improve your health and your life.

Fully Checked

Let's go back to the basics and celebrate Virgo's pure love of cleaning things up. Yes, yes, yes. Today, let's go ahead and organize, sort, clean, purify, cleanse, edit, and scrub. Let's label the different sections of our junk drawer. Categorize, analyze, systematize. Let's do whatever we need to do to breathe an inner sigh of relief. Let's clean our desks, answer fifty emails, return phone calls. Let's even make time for a few yoga stretches or 10 minutes of meditation. And though I love truffle fries, today I might let a good hearty salad win the day. It's spring cleaning in September, let's clean up on all levels—physical, emotional, and mental. Let's not forget those bags we've been meaning to take to Goodwill. Let's add a little Pisces to the equation and whistle while we work. We don't need to be taskmasters. We're just good people who love a fully checked off to-do list.

INVITATION

Alexandra Franzen has a whole wonderful book about making a good checklist. It's called *The Checklist Book* and it is the most compassionate approach to checklists I've ever read. Buy it and dive into checklist deliciousness!

Virgo

Free-Flowing Artistry

Virgo can easily trigger plenty of free-floating anxiety. Instead, I invite us to welcome free-flowing artistry. And on that note, let's explore a few ways to transform anxiety into artistry. Let's start with the breath. Always start there. Let's take a few deep breaths and feel our feet on the earth. Let's feel our goodness seeping into the earth and the earth's blessing seeping into us. Let's allow our loving hands to tenderly touch our own body. We can say hello to the heart. Hello, belly. Hello, furrowed brow. We can soothe ourselves with kind mama hands. We can drink a warm beverage and wrap our hands around the cup or listen outside ourselves. We can listen inside ourselves. Let's walk and stop before beauty, breathe it in. Let's hum ourselves a love song or a lullaby. We can write for 15 minutes without stopping or take a long shower and wear something we love. Let's breathe some more. Let's eat a crunchy apple and let's list everything that has gone right today. Let's trust organic timing and walk through any door and say, "Fresh start!"

INVITATION

Make that list: "Everything that has gone right today."

Staying Open

It's easy to walk into a room in our house and see something that needs to be fixed. We might see everything that is broken or out of place or dirty or that needs attention. But perhaps instead of doing anything about it, we just add it to our list of to-dos and we carry that list in our head everywhere, and it begins to weigh us down. I encourage us instead to walk into a room and see tulips on a gorgeous table, the collage we made on the wall, our smiling child, how the light creates a prism through the window. This isn't a gratitude list exactly. This is about where we choose to put our attention. It's not to ignore the mess, but it's a whole lot easier to address the mess when we feel open and ready to receive goodness. Let's stay open to the beauty and bounty in our lives today.

INVITATION

Instead of fixing, try this: Make a little altar in your home to celebrate someone you love. It might just be a fresh flower and a picture, but it's a small moment of beauty to be cherished.

Virgo

Tiny Devotions

Let's think of today as a day of tiny devotions. Virgo precisely and lovingly attends to the beauty and efficiency of the physical world. It pays attention to all the small gestures we offer one another throughout the day. We can pour coffee, shake someone's hand, plant a seed or say hello—all with attention, care, and presence. Virgo says God or grace or love is in the details. We create a culture of love and connection through our tiny devoted acts, thoughts, and offerings. Bold action and grand gestures are important too. But today let us devote ourselves to offering our love in the simplest, purest, quietest ways.

INVITATION

What are your tiny love offerings? I might pour a glass of water for my husband without him asking, or water the plants in my backyard after a long day. I might give my daughter a hand rub or invite my son on a little walk and talk around the block. Think about how you can offer your love in a small way today.

Virgo Friends

Here are the reasons it's great to have a Virgo friend:

1. They will take care of, and help you take care of, your physical, emotional, and mental well-being.

2. They will find you the best doctors, healers, counselors, hairdressers, designers, you name it. They can hook you up with excellence.

3. They will not let you go anywhere looking anything less than your best self. Need to choose the perfect outfit for a specific occasion? Call your Virgo friend.

4. They are often very practical and analytical and can help you sort through any issue.

5. They have amazing editorial eyes. They know how to refine and improve just about anything.

6. They work harder than pretty much any sign in the zodiac and will work hard with you if you have something important that needs to get done.

7. They have tons of devotion and love and would do just about anything for their near and dear.

8. If you want to feel and be healthier and need a partner on that quest, call your Virgo pal for yoga, a healthy lunch, and the latest and best supplement.

9. They love dogs and cats and other sweet, small creatures and are their champions.

Celebrate your Virgo friends today!

INVITATION

Reach out to your Virgo pals today to tell them how much you love them and why!

You've Got This

Virgo wakes up from the Leo summer party and says, "It's time to get to work." She says, "What are we waiting for?" Virgo is devoted to good work, well done. Virgo also says, "Whatever issue or problem or obstruction might stand in the way of your good work, we can figure it out." Virgo is incredibly capable and smart and no-nonsense. Virgo's rallying cry is, "You've got this! Just put on some scrappy work clothes and clean out that base- ment, closet, or shed. Throw away the Twinkies and make yourself a morning smoothie. Tackle that first step and you'll be on your way." Virgo says, "Follow me. I'm out to improve the world. First stop: yoga class." Virgo infuses us all with the hope and the truth that we can all be healthier and more devoted to the work that is ours to do.

INVITATION

If you haven't moved your body in a while, just decide that you will stretch today. That's it. Just stretch for 5 minutes. A little move- ment leads to more movement within and without.

Macro Appreciation

Virgos often feel that they are the only ones who could possibly create order and keep the world running. Virgos might feel, for instance, that if they are not paying attention, the ocean might dry up. As with any sign, we have to look to the sign opposite for balance and relief. So anytime we get too analytical or critical under Virgo, we have to call in the spaciousness and flow and big picture of Pisces. It's too easy to list all our imperfections and shortcomings under Virgo. We have to remember to look up and out, breathe, and trust that we are a part of something much greater at work today. Try macro appreciation instead of micromanagement today. Add devotion, sensuality, and trust to your work ethic today. Clean if you are called to do so, but only if you are blasting your favorite music through the house as you do. So today, try to do work that you love or bring love to the work that you do.

INVITATION

Try to catch yourself when you've been attending to the minutiae too long. Look up and out! Just find the horizon, breathe, and remember the big wide world.

Virgo

A Job Well Done

Give a Virgo work that is true to who she is and she will not cease until the project is done perfectly. Virgo, refines, purifies, collects, and systematizes information. Virgo cleans, organizes, and improves. She stays on course and on task and uses her keen eye to hone in on what does not yet meet the grade. Sometimes Virgo energy is exhausting because we require so much of ourselves and others. And still, we often feel like we fall short. But some days Virgo feels delicious because there is no better sign when it comes to really doing a job well. There is no better sign to clean up our act and start to feel better about ourselves—our health and our work in the world. Under Virgo, we make healthier choices. And once we boot our inner critic out the door, we stop procrastinating and dive into the first task at hand. And that feels great.

INVITATION

Try writing "No" at the top of your page. Start there. No to what? Write for 10 minutes. Now write "Yes" and do the same.

Virgo Is Sexy

This is just a little heads-up that Virgo can be very sexy. Why? Because Virgo knows specifically what it likes and specifically what it does not like. And when a Virgo really loves something, she's devoted and meticulously attentive. So even though Scorpio and Taurus and even Aries and Libra get a lot of attention for sexuality, sensuality, and the love of the relationship dance, Virgo is quietly steamy and wholly into what turns her on. Virgos love nothing more than their work, but they also quietly love many things only a few will know about. When in Virgo, we can all ask ourselves about pleasure. What do we really like, and how can we invite more of it into our lives? Here are some sultry Virgos to give us the vibe: Beyoncé, Lauren Bacall, Sean Connery, Freddie Mercury.

INVITATION

Let's write:

My sexuality is like . . .

My love is like . . .

Write for 10 minutes about each.

Soothing To-Dos and Good News

Here's another Virgo to-do list:

1. Make a scrumptious breakfast.
2. Stay in bed longer than usual.
3. Read a poem out loud.
4. Get outside sometime in the morning and take three deep breaths. Look at the sky.
5. Wear something cozy.
6. Refuse *should*.
7. Stretch.
8. Make something—a collage, a poem, scones.
9. Hug something soft.
10. Write a real snail-mail letter.
11. Collect all the loose change in the house and start a piggy bank.
12. Buy flowers.

INVITATION

Let's add something to our to-do list: "Share the good news." Whenever we start to create the inner list of worries, let's remind ourselves of the good news of our lives. The good news is that we woke up this morning. The good news is that the world is starting to flower. The good news is . . . If you feel extra inspired, try using this as a writing prompt!

Beautifier

What if each and every one of us were a beautifier? What if we took that mission quite seriously? Everyday is a chance to beautify, refine, improve, and repeat. What if we showed up in a humble and helpful way to create more beauty in our daily living? It requires a kind of devotion, and Virgo is most certainly devoted. How might we each add or realize beauty in our lives today?

INVITATION

Try this: Close your eyes and listen for what requires your meticulous and devoted attention today. Organizing your sock drawer might leap to mind first, but let's go deeper. Do you need to devote yourself to your creative life? Once you decide, remember that you are a beautifier. Hold this thought as you journey through your day.

Virgo

I Know How to Fix This

Let's ask ourselves where and how we want to apply our unique intelligence. Ask, "What am I smart about and how can I help?" Or, "I know how to fix this, and this is mine to fix." Virgo asks us to take responsibility for cleaning our own room. It asks that we use our discernment in all communication, that we find a better way to make things better in our word and deed. Virgo is willing to work hard; and Virgo loves good work. If ever there were a time to apply our unique intelligence to good work on behalf of us all, it's now. How can we each up our game with devotion, love, and clear action? Let's do it. Let's begin again today.

INVITATION

Sometime today, make a quick little list. At the top, write: "I can fix this." Don't choose gigantic things to fix; just start with the lightbulb that's out in the closet. But fix it—because you can.

Babies

Virgo itself is a great sign of motherhood. It will do almost anything to care for the health and welfare of its babies. And by the
way, for a Virgo, babies absolutely include the entire animal king-
dom. There are also many Virgos who invest their most devotional
mother energy in work. They improve, refine, and edit what exists,
implementing systems that help everything run with greater ease.
Today, let us be grateful for the mother energy in our lives and, as
ever, be a good mama to ourselves.

INVITATION

Did you know that Virgo rules dogs and cats? It is one of the great
signs connected to our animal friends. Spend some time today
thinking about the gifts that the animals in your life give you. Why
is the angel-that-is-your-dog in your life?

Altars

A poem I wrote:

Make of your day an altar
And with great care
Place what you wish to honor
At its center.

Make of your day an altar
and give it
the flower of your attention,
The fullness of your presence.

Make this day an altar.
Offer your love
To its hurried minutes
And pressing hours.

Make of this day
A living altar.
Feel the blessing
It bestows upon you.
Stand before it
Ready to begin.

INVITATION

Sometime today, make an altar. Walk in nature and collect some items to create an altar or light a candle and place a picture of someone you love. Visit Day Shildkret's www.morningaltars.com for wonderful ideas to get you started.

Harmlessness

Under Virgo, we can consciously choose harmlessness and right speech. We can catch ourselves before we list all our corrections and grievances. We can also first try to stand in a place of love before we offer our analysis. Virgo wants things to be clean, pure, refined, and perfect, so beauty and grace can present with ease. But always we have to remember why we are perfecting and correcting, and start with the beauty of the whole before we dissect. Let's try to serve and see with love before we offer, inwardly or outwardly, our refinements.

INVITATION

Try to spend this day without complaining or speaking disparagingly about anyone else.

Body Blessing

Virgo rules everything it takes to get sober. It tends to the well-being of the body and works to treat the body as a temple. Of course, there's a great journey with Virgo. At first, Virgo can list all the ways it is broken or doesn't measure up. But when Virgo opens to its opposite and receives the unconditional love and the oceans of compassion from Pisces, it can unfold in exquisite ways. Virgo can refine and improve just about anything. She can devote herself to health on all levels. Under Virgo, we get well. We heal. We celebrate our well-being.

INVITATION

Read Jan Richardson's poem "Blessing for the Body" slowly and out loud.

Honoring Virgo

If we were to honor Virgo today, we'd begin with silence and spaciousness. We'd begin with a deep breath or two, and we'd draw a card from a tarot deck or we'd light a candle with intention. We might make a cup of tea and sit calmly while we drink it. Yoga is always delicious on a Virgo day as well. We'd eat with awareness and we'd eat something we know our bodies would love. We might take some time to clean or organize an area of our home. We might bake bread. We might notice if we are anxious or agitated and, if so, make some choices to create perspective and flow. The ocean, a bath, a river walk, a poem? Most importantly, we'd remember to talk to ourselves with kindness.

INVITATION

Before we shift our attention to Libra, let's look back at the month and note what has changed. Did Virgo help you to grow? Did you refine or improve or bring greater health to an area of your life? Were you able to do some of the work you feel you are here to do? Let's reflect.

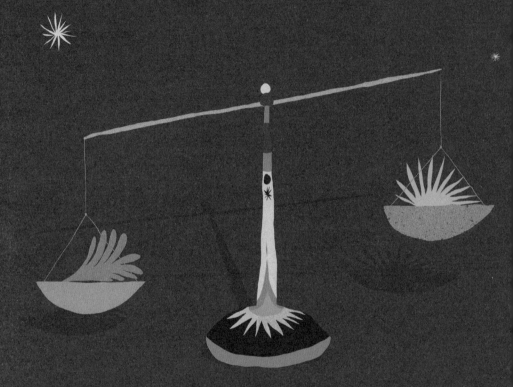

Libra

Welcoming Libra

Today, we look up from our tireless Virgo work and see another face. We offer our hand, our cheek to kiss. We say, "Hello! How about coffee?" We remember that we are the hosts of our own life party and if we want to have a good time, we better start conversing with our guests and make sure that there's good food and cozy places to sit. Libra is the sign of relationships. It's also the sign of beauty, balance, and diplomacy. We yearn for, fight for, stand for peace under Libra and will do just about anything to achieve those ideals. We stand for fairness and justice and work so that we may all learn to treat one another with greater kindness and integrity. Under Libra we want to connect, collaborate, and be together. We want to dance the dance of connection. And always, always under Libra, we want to let beauty lead the way. We name the beautiful even in what another would find ugly. We look deeper.

INVITATION

Sometime today, stop. Notice something beautiful in nature, in your environment, or in another human being. Breathe it in. Begin to let beauty work on you.

Libra List

Here are a few ideas about how to spend a Libra day:

Go on a lunch date with someone you love.

Stay in bed with someone you love.

Take yourself on a beauty walk.

Do a house project that makes you sigh with pleasure once it's complete.

Do laundry and take the clothes out while they are still warm and hold the warm clothes and feel that deliciousness and then fold them in no hurry.

Take yourself to an art gallery or an art-house movie in the middle of the day. Get popcorn.

Write a love letter to yourself or your love or a friend or a future love.

Make a five-year plan with colorful markers, lots of doodles, and a great number of exclamation points.

Stand up for someone that needs your support.

Offer your big love.

INVITATION

Choose any one of the above suggestions and dive in. Embrace it fully.

Balance Beams

Do you remember trying to walk on a balance beam as a kid? How was it? Libra is a bit like that walk. Each step offers the possibility of balance, or a wobbly dance, or of falling off completely. The walk can be total grace, or it can be a nail-biter. Libra invites us to take each step in integrity and with care. Libra offers that striving for balance is a beautiful thing and that each chosen step forward is our cooperation and trust of the unknown. Libra is already succeeding with the first step out of indecision. With each and every step we can find balance and beauty anew.

INVITATION

It gets harder and harder to physically balance as we get older. But it's very good to practice. Our own outer equilibrium can affect our inner state as well. Certain yoga poses are great for practicing balance. And if you really want to be simple about it, just stand on one leg for a bit and practice finding that sweet balanced spot.

Libra

On the Level

Libra isn't always the most effusive of signs. It can be quite cool and dispassionate, but it stands for evolving the way we treat one another. It is impossible for most of us to stand as love in every encounter, but can we lean in that direction? Can we intensely dislike someone and yet practice making a conscious fair choice about how we respond to them? It's so easy to react immediately and sometimes unconsciously to what we don't like. How do we choose the next best step for ourselves and others? Libra asks us not to rise above or cower below in our interactions. It asks that we attempt to meet on the level, honoring our sovereign self and attempting to see the light in another. It's our greatest work, learning how to receive one another and encourage greater wisdom in one another. It's impossibly difficult, but we can't give up. Too much is at stake.

INVITATION

Read the poem "Out of a Great Need" by Hafiz. Read it slowly and out loud.

Co-creation

Libra ultimately is about how we choose to see and treat one another. It's honoring our differences but feeling our oneness. It is not about merging or yielding or giving up one's needs or differences to make a relationship work. It is not about codependency. It is about co-creation. We listen, see, dialogue with the other and in so doing, we feel the other is not the other, but another soul like us. Libra asks us to search for common ground, to find what is decent or good or humane or even beautiful in another and do what we can to connect from that place. Under Libra, we all have the opportunity to play the role of host or diplomat, peacemaker or lover. The choices we each make leave beauty or chaos in our wake. Libra is the sign of choice. How do we each choose to connect? How do we each choose to create moments of peace?

INVITATION

Think about your circle of friends or your workmates. Now think about someone in that circle that you know you have something to offer. Call to mind someone you know you could help. Now, think about someone in your circle who definitely has a gift for you, someone from whom you could learn something important. Now promise yourself to pursue the deepening of both relationships.

Libra

Dynamic Duos

Think of Fred and Ginger, Lennon and McCartney, Paul Allen and Bill Gates, The Indigo Girls, Billie Eilish and Finneas, Helen Keller and Annie Sullivan, Ben and Jerry, Beyoncé and Jay-Z, Lucy and Ethel, Batman and Robin, Pippin and Jordan, Bogart and Bacall, Tina Fey and Amy Poehler. Every dynamic duo is ruled by Libra. Every dynamic duo needs the other for balance, inspiration, passion, and motivation. Every dynamic duo has a gift to give together.

INVITATION

On this Libra day, reach out to your partner in crime, best buddy, the person or people who raise you up and help you give the best of yourself. Shout out the partnerships that help you thrive.

Uranus

Uranus is the harbinger of the new. Uranus wakes us up and teaches us to relate in new and more progressive ways. In Libra, Uranus is the soul-centered ruler that says "Love who you love. See only the soul in another. Shake out your old inner laws about how we treat or meet one another. Meet one another through the eyes of the soul." Uranus is also connected to Aquarius and encourages us all to open our eyes to the power of community. Beautiful and potent communities form when we honor each member and let our differences strengthen the whole. Under Uranus, we can make a choice that defies old ways. We can reinvent what it is to relate. We can honor what makes us each unique but not let our differences be barriers.

INVITATION

Uranus always welcomes experimentation. It wants us to shake up our lives and see with fresh eyes. Make things new today: try taking a different route to work; start your day with 5 minutes of meditation instead of immediately checking your phone. Make a few surprising choices.

Libra

Notice

What do we choose to say? What do we choose *not* to say? When do we choose to keep the peace? And when do we choose to speak up and disrupt it in the name of justice or fairness? Libra loves balance and harmony, so does not readily jump into conflict. But even for the peace-loving Libra, there are times when a false peace must be challenged to bring true healing. Let's take some time today to get a little perspective and observe our own process about when we choose to speak up or stay silent.

INVITATION

Let's notice the choices we make today. Notice if you allow your whole authentic self, along with your true needs and desires, to be a part of your choices. Notice when you accommodate or appease, when you'd rather not. Notice the choices that feel nourishing and, likewise, notice the choices that diminish your light or deplete you. To affect true change, you must first take stock of where you are.

How Are You, Self?

Libra rules the dance of relationships. The first and primary relationship is with the self. Are you in conversation with the self that wants the best for you, the one that wants to see you thrive? Or have you been ignoring that voice, listening instead to the bully critic on your shoulder? Today, have a Libran conversation with that soul self. She might say something like this, "Hey there, good morning. How are you? You didn't sleep so well? It's going to be OK. Just start the day gently. You know what? You're doing a good job. You are. Times are tough. I'm proud of you. Just do the next tiny thing you have to do today. Maybe you can even ask for a little help; take a breath. Now make a cup of tea. Don't just try to get through the day. Let yourself be surprised or, yes, even delighted by something today. Go easy. I know you've got this."

INVITATION

We often give free license to our inner critic but leave no room for a voice of kindness. It's only fair to check in with both. What would the kindest voice say to you today? What would your favorite teacher offer you as counsel? Allow those words to have a space in your life and in your heart today.

Go In

If it's not working on the outside, go in. That is, if your relationships are feeling out of sorts or everyone is making you a little crazy, or even if just one person is driving you nuts, spend some time on the relationship with yourself. Get really quiet, take a walk, close your eyes, breathe in a way that returns you to yourself, and then start to peel away the layers of blame or sadness or anger. Keep digging deep. Eventually when we shed these layers, we reach something very tender and vulnerable and aching. Libra asks us to befriend that part of yourself. Create a relationship with that uncertain, quivering self. Be ever so tender and kind within. Then look up and out into the world with softer eyes.

INVITATION

There are myriad ways to "go in." You might journal, walk, meditate. You could have a dear friend witness you as you try to articulate the pain. You can spend time in nature. Listen to your favorite piece of music and dream. Dive deep to emerge with clarity.

Open and Willing

On this Libran day, I wish for you a good day. I wish for you a day of feeling at ease, balanced, and quiet inside. I hope that kindness knocks on your door today. I wish you many moments of appreciation for the relationships in your life. I hope you have a chance to offer your kindness. I hope you have a chance to say, "And who are you? I'm interested in you." I hope you allow yourself to be imperfectly perfect and wobbly in all the right ways. On this Libran day, may we all make good choices, choices that grow our light. May we seek to do no harm. Let's have a good day, friends. Let's bring ourselves to the day open and willing.

INVITATION

Take a centering, quieting moment today before you rush out into the world. Make a few wishes, prayers, and intentions for yourself.

Libra

Walk in Beauty

Libra rules beauty within and without. We can name beauty, breathe beauty, excavate beauty. Today, we can feel our own unique power to manifest our own offerings of beauty. Today, look for the beauty beneath the obvious, for hidden beauty. Look for beauty that masquerades as what we might name ugly. Spend enough time with someone or something until you drop deeply into the beauty yearning to emerge. May we walk in beauty, as beauty, offering the beautiful.

INVITATION

I often think about what I leave "in my wake." That is, when I am in a space and then leave that space, what do I leave behind? I like to think that I leave beauty in my wake. What does that mean to you? Think about leaving beauty in your wake today, or finding beauty as you go.

Tango

Today, we welcome partnership, collaboration, and a renewed desire to work together. Sometimes in the struggles of our lives, we isolate or close down. We try to manage pain or fear on our own. We forget to reach out, ask for help, tell our story. We forget others are struggling too. That's why we need to remember to tell our stories, to ask our questions out loud, to risk vulnerability, to listen and respond. Libra teaches about exchange, give and take, collaboration and choice. We actually have to choose to play and create and work together. We offer our talents to help a friend. We invite a friend to help us. Offer your hand or heart. Invite the beauty of the dance in work or love into your life. Now is not a time to dance solo. I'm thinking a tango or a little fifties swing.

INVITATION

Help a friend achieve one of their goals. Help them study. Introduce them to another friend who could be of assistance. Ask for similar help yourself!

Tiny Love Protests

As a sign of peace on March 25, 1969, over fifty years ago, John Lennon and Yoko Ono climbed into bed with a sign above them that said "Bed Peace." This protest was one of many that asked us to make love, not war. John and Yoko had just married five days earlier. They created the soundtrack for the "bed-in" with "Give Peace a Chance." (Lennon was a Libra and Ono has a Libra ascendant.) So on this Libra day, I ask all of us to protest with a little peace, beauty, and love. How can we each sound a note that drowns out the ugly, the fractious, the polarizing. What might we do as tiny love protests? Twelve years ago, a group of friends and I stood on street corners all over Los Angeles and eventually the United States with signs that said, "Hello, love." We greeted anyone who walked or drove by with those words. What happens when we greet one another with love? What happens when we acknowledge the love that we are? Any act of beauty or peacemaking is a potent act. Any act of kindness or love is a transformational act. Any offering of light begins to eliminate the darkness. Let's make this Libran day a little revolutionary with our many love protests and our radical offerings of light.

INVITATION

What's your tiny, revolutionary act of love for today?

Our Libra Friends

Here are the reasons it's great to have a Libra friend:

1. They have an eye for beauty. They will introduce you to all things beautiful.

2. They are fair, just, and diplomatic. They will stand up and speak out about how we treat one another.

3. They will make sure you have everything you need. They will check in with you often to see how you are. It is a great joy for a Libra to take good care of their people.

4. They are peacemakers. They want us all to live in harmony. They are the ultimate diplomats.

5. They are great conversationalists.

6. They will always weigh things carefully before they make a decision.

7. They stand for the true, the noble, and the good.

8. They love *love*, whether romantic or loving friend-ship. They give themselves to love.

9. They love the law and will always uphold what they know to be beautiful and good.

10. They are kind and graceful, peaceful and appreciative.

Yay for our Libra friends!

INVITATION

Reach out to your Libra friends to tell them you love them and why!

How Are You? How Am I?

Libra asks, "How are you? What do you think? Do you agree? What would you like to do? Is there any way I can help you?" Libra brings total engagement to the other. To balance the scales, call in the energy of Aries and ask the same questions, "What do I think? How am I? What would I like to do? Is there any way I can help myself?" This isn't selfishness. It's just reclaiming a bit of the Libra energy often used to make everything nice. When Libra is in balance and releases itself from worrying about everyone else, then Libra can bring great social change, beautiful design, and incredibly stimulating conversation. So when in Libra, wine and dine yourself, ask yourself beautiful questions all day long; and only then, with a full cup, connect.

INVITATION

Pause this very moment and check in. Ask yourself: "How am I?" And then again, "No really, how am I?" Answer at the deepest level you can in this moment. Write if that's helpful. You can start with the prompt, "Let me tell you how I am . . ."

Swan

In water, swans are the most elegant and peaceful creatures. On land, they waddle in a kind of awkward fashion, struggling to find the ease and grace of their native element. I think many of us have a whole host of swan-out-of-water moments throughout our day, and then feel the precious relief of being in our element now and then. Libra invites us to notice those at-peace moments. It invites us to notice when we are lumbering and out of sorts and then when we manage to find the current that carries us. It also reminds us that there are beautiful choices presented again and again, throughout a day, throughout a life. There's always a more graceful choice. Let's practice choosing it.

INVITATION

Read Rainer Maria Rilke's poem "The Swan." Read it out loud and slowly!

Libra

Walking and Talking

Would you like to take a walk? Come with me. I have so many questions I'd like to ask you. How are you, my friend? How is your heart? Have you been carrying a lot these days? Is there anything you can put down for a time? I wonder when do you feel most at peace in your element, in your skin? I'd love to hear about one of those moments, those peaceful inhabited times. What have you been thinking about lately? What's on your mind? Is there something you've been carrying quietly that wants to be said aloud? Are you stopping now and then to fully breathe in your life? I hope so. Are you yearning? What for? Are you longing? What for? Are you full with something? What with? What do you love wholeheartedly? How can you give yourself more deeply to that? I would love to hear any words you'd like to share. I'm glad you are walking with me.

INVITATION

Share some of the answers to the questions above in your journal. Once you're done, read some of those answers to a friend.

In Love, Here and Now

Regardless of whether or not we have a partner, we can all practice choosing love. Many who do have partners don't spend enough time in love. We could all stand in love many more moments of the day. What does that look like? Listening, touching, tasting, breathing, noticing, appreciating, celebrating. What else does that look like? Offering up words of love, care, kindness for yourself and all you meet? We can never go wrong offering our love. Make tiny gestures and make bold ones. Love a flower. Love your dog. Love yourself. But stand in the current of love. It is ever-present and ever-beckoning. How do you wish to make it a day to remember?

INVITATION

Are you in love? Let your love know it. Are you falling in love? Fall deeper. Do you want to be in love? Then choose to be in love here and now with yourself, with someone who brings beauty to your life.

Libra

Both/And

Libra offers a both/and approach to peace. It goes like this. I am both angry and willing to take a few deep, calming breaths. I am both sad and willing to sit calmly with the sadness, trusting it will change. Or, I am both furious with that person and willing to listen more deeply and talk rationally about why I am angry. We shouldn't repress, ignore, or silence the big chaotic feelings, but we don't have to give them the full say. Anger can ride with us in the front seat and compassion can whisper from the back. Don't dismiss the unrest. Just let it converse with beauty or inspiration or breath. Allow the conversation, allow the cooperation.

INVITATION

There is something deeply calming about naming the both/and. Try writing a few of these sentences yourself. Hold the paradox.

Set Things Straight

Have you been meaning to make a phone call, send an email, invite someone to talk? Has an emotional issue been building up that needs to be addressed? Today, we can all bring a little more clarity and detachment to difficult interactions. There may still be some tough emotional moments, but Libra is fair and reasonable and even a little detached in a healthy way. Use today to set things straight and allow for a fresh start. And this applies to how we all have been treating ourselves lately too. Do we need a reboot? Do we need to listen within a little more carefully? Are we neglecting our own inner voice, need, yearning? Libra allows for grace and balance when we address any underlying difficulty. Let's initiate a little healing in our relationships.

INVITATION

Today, offer an open hand. When the hand is clenched or stuffed into a pocket, we are not available to a healing dialogue. An open hand, both physically and metaphorically, makes it possible to converse. We open our hand when we shake hands or hug. Today, offer your open hand and see what can be resolved.

Strongly Spoken

Sometimes Libra doesn't feel like such a peaceful sign. Many of the world's greatest war generals have been Libras. Interesting, yes? Yes, Libra is indeed a sign of peace, but it is peace reached through the willingness to address conflict. We don't want false peace or an imitation of peace in ourselves or in the world. We want to address the challenges, inequities, and pain that prevent harmonious living. Libra asks us to choose the peaceful path, step by step avoiding huge reactivity. And Libra does absolutely stand for what is fair, just, decent, and equitable. So when in Libra, let's also ask ourselves what might need to be strongly spoken into the world to bring us a step closer to real peace within our own often warring humanity.

INVITATION

Sometimes we need to strategize for peace. What truly is necessary to bring warring opposites together? What compromises must be struck? What patience is necessary? Call upon all your wisdom, justice, and listening skills if there is something to be resolved. Come forth in the name of collaboration and cooperation.

Choose a Few People

Let's think of three people in our lives. What is one small thing we can do in each relationship that might make it better? That is, is there anything we might offer or adjust that would allow greater ease to be present? Is there anything we can do that might make the relationship brighter, sweeter? Is there someone that actually needs the particular care we know we can offer? Maybe it's simply a phone call or a card sent by mail. Maybe we share our gratitude or find a way to help behind the scenes. Maybe we ask some good questions and are willing to fully listen.

INVITATION

Choose a few people and try to change the course of their day for the better. Can you soothe or brighten, calm or encourage? You can deepen or strengthen a connection. Help someone carry something heavy today. Look up and out and extend love.

Libra

On the Other Hand

Today, I'd like to offer a very Libran phrase: "On the other hand . . ."
We seem, as humanity, to have grown more and more adamant
about things. We are rooted in our sides and opinions so deeply
that we cannot be swayed by any form of discussion. Just as an
experiment today, if we find ourselves declaring what we consider an absolute truth like: "They are idiots," or "Any sane person
would know," or "That is wrong and this is right," let's follow
that thought with the phrase "on the other hand" and see what
emerges. Make some space for "on the other hand" and it might
just open a tiny door for compassion or discussion or bridge
building.

INVITATION

Let's write. Write something that feels like a truth to you and then
see what happens if you follow that with "on the other hand . . ."

The Market

Recently, I went to buy fish at the market, and the man who waited on me could not have been more lovely. We chatted about my upcoming dinner with friends and he wished me a beautiful weekend. On the way out, I held the door for a woman entering and she said, "Thank you very much, young lady." Then I continued on to the grocery store, where a nice guy getting on a scooter in the parking lot smiled a huge, genuine smile. I thought, What a sweet hour it's been. I'm feeling better than I have in quite a while. And I thought, *Thank goodness for small kindnesses and warmth from strangers*. Thank goodness. Any day is a day we can reset, start again, summon hope. Thank goodness there are many good humans who wish to be generous, connected, and curious. Offer a smile, a nod, a kind gesture, and be open to receive one as well.

INVITATION

Notice kind gestures offered. Do not let them pass. Receive them fully. Consciously offer up your own.

Libra

Beauty Liberates

Venus and Uranus are two planets deeply connected to Libra. Venus says, "Spend the day doing what you value. Steep in what you consider beautiful. Enjoy others. Gather for pleasure." Uranus says, "Try something new, shake loose, let go, choose freedom." Together, they might say, "Let people, including yourself, love who and what they love. Appreciate how beauty liberates us from darkness. Allow others the freedom we want for ourselves." Together they say, "See the beauty in who you are. Name it. For this day, free yourself from your flavor of inner criticism. Choose to find beauty within."

INVITATION

There is a beautiful children's book by Barbara Cooney called *Miss Rumphius*. In it, Alice, a little girl, remembers her grandfather who lived by the sea and traveled to many foreign lands. Alice says she too wants to travel and live by the sea when she is older. Her grandfather says, "But you must do a third thing." Alice asks what that is. He says, "You must do something to make the world more beautiful." Your invitation today is simply to read this book!

Weighing Options

Libra is a sign that always weighs its options. On any given day, a Libra can swing from one definite decision to the exact opposite. But there is a weight to indecision; it can be absolutely anxiety producing, swinging from one side to another over and over again. Libra grows when it makes a tiny decision and acts on that decision. Making a series of tiny decisions can help us to finally arrive at the big conclusion.

INVITATION

Write down one or two decisions you need to make in your life. "I need to decide whether or not to take the job." Or "I need to decide if I am moving cross country." Then, brainstorm a few tiny actions you could take that might help you move forward or clarify your path. Make sure some of those actions are tangible physical actions to help you get out of your head.

Libra

Culture of Peace

Every bit of artistry and beauty helps to create a culture of peace. Yes, we need to stand up, fight, speak out, and be heard. We also need to build beauty, harmony, and peace through our authentic creative expression. It might be how we cook a meal, tend to a garden, write a letter. It might be music we play or the music we choose to fill our house. It might be a castle we build out of blocks with a child. The time is now to elevate our consciousness through individual gestures of beauty, offered daily, to create a culture of peace.

INVITATION

Singing together goes a long way toward creating an experience of group peace. It's hopeful. It's so beautiful to hear a group, a choir, a family, or a community make a joyful noise. So find a way to sing today. Even if you think you can't sing, sing. Sing your way into greater harmony. When others are singing, you can listen with your whole heart. Let it melt you a little, and then join in.

Equanimity

Here is the definition of equanimity from the Oxford Dictionary: "mental calmness, composure and evenness of temper, especially in a difficult situation." Equanimity is so very Libran. Today, take as much reflection or meditation time as possible. Attempt to calm the inner seas. Ask inwardly what you need to know to move forward with less strife, obstruction, or conflict. Invite grace. Invite easeful unfolding. Then take some time to send clarifying light and wisdom to those who have important decisions to make this week. Offer light to what is just and true and good.

INVITATION

Think about what would help you feel "mentally calm." Do you need to exercise? Do you need to spend time in nature? Journal? What promotes more ease and composure in your life when the going gets tough? Often, it helps to prepare for how to handle moments of conflict or crisis, so when we are standing in them, we have a choice about how we want to respond.

Libra

Inner Parties

Libra is the ultimate host or hostess, but today let's host our own inner party. Let's consider the ambience. Is it wild and festive or a small, quiet celebration? Who shall we invite? Who would add beauty and goodness to this inner party? What about music? What's the soundtrack today? And what will we eat? Libra spends so much time attending to the needs of others that it sometimes forgets its own inner life. So on this Libran day, let's allow this inner party to be in honor of each of us. What brings the most joy? How can we amplify that? Let's give ourselves full permission to throw the kind of party that feels deeply nourishing. Today is an ordinary day, but heightened by our own secret celebrations. I think my party has to have guacamole, lots of poetry, and bountiful flowers. I'd love for it to feel like a daylong gourmet picnic.

INVITATION

Create an actual invitation to your inner party. Invite yourself. Give yourself a sense of what might unfold and then ask for your own RSVP. Say yes.

Approaching Scorpio

When in Libra, it is easier to summon grace, kindness, and diplomacy. We extend ourselves to others with greater ease, and conversations flow. We are more willing to search for common . ground. But as we approach the sign of Scorpio, it is worth noting that Libra has a tendency to be overly polite in the name of peace. If we plaster an accommodating smile over inner resentment or unrest, we are not creating peace. If we are polite, charming, and nice while seething inside, we are making matters worse. Libra gives us the chance to make the decision to share and discuss what matters and what needs to be addressed. Our friend Scorpio will always give us the push to do exactly that. If we have been assessing the situation too long, Scorpio will nudge us into deeper, healing waters.

INVITATION

Is there a relationship in your life that has been on pause or has not been addressed when it clearly needs to be? Start to take some healing steps. Prepare to make the call, send the email, or ask for a meeting.

Scorpio

Welcoming Scorpio

Today, we welcome Scorpio—a sign of great strength and depth. Scorpio wrestles. It stays in the ring. It never gives up. Scorpio penetrates, researches, and digs into the deepest dark. It holds on until it achieves victory or gets to the heart of the mystery or establishes the intimacy it craves. Scorpio's strength is in its tenacity—its holding power. It sees things through and it sees *through* anything that lacks truth or depth. Use Scorpio to dig in, commit, or penetrate. Use Scorpio to stand alongside your fear and walk forward, acknowledging it, but not giving it the upper hand. Use Scorpio to stand for and fight for what you value. Use Scorpio to speak your truth. Sometimes that takes the most courage of all. Finally, use Scorpio to name what pains you so you can begin to heal. Remember, Scorpio rules death *and* rebirth.

INVITATION

Every morning, we sit up and take our first upright breath. This is a moment to begin again. Put your hand on your heart and remember the strength that ever resides within you. Feel the power that is untapped and available to you at any time to work your way through any troubles.

A Line in the Sand

Under Scorpio, we sometimes reach a breaking point. This isn't necessarily a bad thing. If we've been weighing things under Libra, we make a strong decision under Scorpio. We draw a line in the sand. We say, "Enough." We summon our inner warrior and do what needs to be done. It's important to say that these decisions must be made in the light of day with clarity and wisdom. They cannot be reactive or vengeful. This arises when we know that something must and will be addressed that can lead to healing or transformation. Battles must be fought inwardly and outwardly, but those battles are so that light and love can prevail. Scorpio calls upon us to use our strength—physical, emotional, mental, spiritual, and financial to support what is decent, inclusive, and for the good of the whole. What will we stand for? What will we fight for?

INVITATION

Let's write. Put the word "Enough" at the top of the page and write for 15 minutes. Where have you reached a breaking point? Where do you need to draw a line in the sand?

Everything Is Evolving

Scorpio is a sign of great wrestling. Waves of sadness move through, or anger rears its head. Sometimes we feel frustrated or silent in our struggle. But Scorpio also invites us to remember that there are always riches below the surface. The sword of truth glimmers in the darkness. The intense heat of transformation creates gold. Dark, turbulent waters give way to blue. Nothing remains frozen or stuck. Everything is evolving. Even our most intense feelings and reactions will fade and there will be a renewed space of possibility and tender growth. So if we wake sad, let us say there is sadness in this moment, but trust that it is in the process of becoming something else. If we wake up angry, let us say this is anger, but I am not this anger. It is moving through. It is fiery, but I can channel it. I can breathe through it.

INVITATION

Let's write:"I am not this anger" or "I am not this sadness." See where it leads.

The Lake

Come with me friends. We are going to walk along the lake. First, we will walk to a wooded path where the roots of the trees are exposed and worn from all who have crossed. It is a path nestled so close to the lake that we could step off and wade in. Many have. Look at the little duck families. Look at the light, dancing on the water, changing every moment. Now there is a big rock we can sit on with a view of the entire lake. We can wonder about who lives in the little red house across the way. We can dream of all who have walked this path before us. We can notice that time is slowing and expanding even as we sit and look. Then, come with me to a grove of pine trees. It will take ten minutes to get there, and we'll be a little breathless when we arrive, but so happy we have come. We will stand together in this sacred grove wanting to spontaneously say a prayer of gratitude for this very moment, gratitude to have walked together.

INVITATION

Let's write. Start with: "Come with me friends . . ." and then take us on your own specific, magical journey.

Midnight

Let's breathe in the hush of darkness. Let's remember the stillness and depth of midnight. Let's invoke the mysteries of the
self and celebrate the fact that we can explore those depths.
When we befriend Scorpio, we befriend a deep dive into the most
precious secrets of ourselves. We are willing to face our fears.
We refuse to stay hidden. We name our hidden pain and love it
into the light of day. Let's use Scorpio as our most trusted ally to
investigate our greatest secrets and yearnings. Let's allow Scorpio to whisper in our ear, reminding us just how powerful we are.

INVITATION

There is a special kind of silence at midnight. Even if you are a
morning person, experiment with what the night has to whisper to
you. Stay up late and journal. Listen when all the house is quiet. Feel
the potency of the night.

Scorpio

Name the Journey

How can we fiercely and potently grow the light? The time is now. Let's name a big feeling—something that may currently be weighing heavily in our lives. How are we feeling at this moment? Then let's name a quality or feeling we'd like to invite in. Then let's name the journey from one state to another. "Today, I journey from numb and collapsed to spontaneous and appreciative." Let's not worry right now how we'll pull this off. Let's just name the journey. Naming is already a kind of liberation.

INVITATION

Take this a bit further and decide what is to be the first step on this journey from one state of being to another. You could say, "I'll start the journey by taking a walk and noticing the beauty of the trees," or "I'll start the journey by stretching for 5 minutes." What's your next step toward a little more light?

Not Just the Blaze

The blaze is all well and good, but don't forget about the shadows, the corners, and the depths. Scorpio begs us to remember that we cannot abandon the parts of ourselves that make us feel vulnerable. We can't repress or stifle what we might consider our less presentable parts. Scorpio says, "You must bring your whole, messy, vulnerable self to the table." When we're in Scorpio, let's converse with the more troubling aspects of ourselves. We have to name the pain, something we would like to heal. This outing of ourselves without condemnation is powerful and necessary. Invite the hidden part of you into conversation. What does she have to say? Listen, and then love her.

INVITATION

These are the first three lines of my poem "I want to tell you":
I want to tell you that I speak of light
Because my body often
Feels like a hard, knotted thing.

Let's use this writing prompt: "I want to tell you." What do you want and need to say?

Scorpio

The Hydra

The struggle of Scorpio is connected with the story of the nine-headed hydra. Each head represents something with which we must wrestle to clear our path to greater light. The heads stand for fear, hatred, pride, and cruelty, to name a few. Each of us must face our own hydra. And each of us probably has one head that looms larger than the others. Let's ask ourselves what feels like one of our greatest obstructions. What ensnares us? Fear looms large for many. Scorpio invites us to explore these shadows, to welcome to our own table what we consider ugly or problematic. It also invites us to ask for help in our healing, to surrender our own individual fight and welcome a greater grace to work through us.

INVITATION

The hydra is only conquered when we fall to our knees and lift it into the light of the day. It doesn't work to try to cut off the heads. This is the therapeutic process. Today, ask for help in naming and surrendering. The month of Scorpio is a powerful month for *any* kind of therapeutic work—bodywork, counseling, writing. Be sure to get the help you need this month.

Something's Gotta Give

Sometimes we feel like something's got to give. At this time, many of us are up against old patterns that no longer serve, and the pressure to transform is real. As humanity, we are equally up against huge necessary changes. It feels like we need a release valve, but in fact this is the time to get in there and stay determined and tenacious. Scorpio actually invites the dance between control and surrender. We do everything we can to make the inner and outer changes. And then there's a necessary letting go, a surrender to the greater currents at work. There's no doubt that these are pressured times and, yes, something's got to give. For today, let's give ourselves a moment to whisper this internally: "I trust I'm changing for the good. I will keep at it."

INVITATION

Say something to a friend or family member that marks how something has changed within you. Acknowledge the shift. "I'm feeling good today." "I feel lighter this week." "I'm changing." It's so important to say these things out loud and have them witnessed and received.

Scorpio

Let Be

Today, let be. What is, is. For this moment, let's acknowledge what we feel and say hello to all its textures. Let's not beat ourselves up for how we feel. Let's sit with it for a while and befriend it. Grief, fatigue, uncertainty, excitement, sadness. Let be. Let's not try to change anything. We are ever evolving. We are ever changing. Nothing is stagnant or static or stuck, even if it appears to be. Let's trust this process, our process, and be kind to ourselves. Let's listen for our own rhythm. Let's soften our gaze, deepen our breath. Wait, what wants to happen next?

INVITATION

Read Mary Oliver's poem "Love Sorrow." Read it slowly and out loud.

Magic Wands

Answer these two questions quickly and without deliberation.
If you had a magic wand and could heal something in yourself
completely and immediately, what would you heal? Trust your first
response. And if you had that same magic wand and could heal
something in humanity completely and immediately, what specifically would you heal? Trust again. Now you have your marching
orders. You don't have a magic wand, but you have your passion,
intensity, fortitude, and willingness. You've also probably been
working on these things already. Let's make a Scorpionic oath
to continue to work. Let's make tiny gestures every day toward
increased freedom and greater life. If our pain is physical and
cannot be completely healed, let's work on everything around
the physical test. Let's work internally and externally, subtly and
concretely, together and alone.

INVITATION

Let's write: "If I had a magic wand, what would I heal in myself completely and immediately? And what would I heal in the world?"

Scorpio

Letting Go

While Scorpio is a sign of great tenacity, it also requires and invites a profound letting go. There's a time under Scorpio when we realize our grip is too tight and we are trying to control too much. Scorpio's intensity takes over, and we try to orchestrate everything and power through or over. But, at a critical moment, we learn that Scorpio is about a necessary surrender, a letting go. We fall to our knees, release our grip, and no longer will ourselves to fight and struggle alone. We ask for help. We allow ourselves to work with an energy greater than our own. We feel cradled by the earth and touched by the light of the sky. We share our inner battle and ask for help for guidance, for love, to lift this weight and help it transform.

INVITATION

Try this simple exercise: While sitting or standing, tighten every muscle in your body. Intensify the grip. Even hold your breath. After about thirty seconds, release completely and take a few deep breaths. Feel the physical "letting go" and it will help with mental areas you need to release.

Gently Waking

Anyone else have morning dread? Dawn heaviness? Daybreak depression? Even when we can point to many things that are good in life, some mornings feel impossibly difficult. Sometimes we hurl ourselves out of bed muttering. Sometimes we put a blanket over our head and curl into even more of a fetal position. Sometimes we sit up, put our feet on the floor, and just try to take a few deep breaths. For parents out there, let's think about how we wake our kids. We might say, "Sweetie, it's 7:00 a.m. I love you." We try to wake them gently. How can we all wake ourselves more gently? Even if we have someone who curls around and kisses us, how can we internally welcome the day with more ease and less stress? How can we begin more lightly?

INVITATION

Nothing changes until we acknowledge and name it. That's why writing is such a healing path. Even one page of truth-telling begins to shift the trajectory of the day. Here is a prompt that might help shift things: "I don't want to tell you . . ."

Scorpio

Our Scorpio Friends

Here are all the reasons it's good to have a Scorpio friend:

1. They are intensely loyal. They do not give up on friendship easily. They will be there for you in dark hours.

2. They're willing to tell you the truth, even when it's uncomfortable.

3. They are stellar examples of never giving up. Just when you think they are down for the count, they stand up and dive in again.

4. If they are your pal, you get to discover that they are actually big, soft, tender creatures under their ferocity.

5. Oh, and speaking of ferocity, they will fight for you even if you think you don't want them to; and they will most often win.

6. They are completely unafraid to navigate the darkest of dark with you and you can relax in their presence because, you know, they've got you.

7. They're willing to shed skins, transform, and heal, and will inspire you to do the same.

Celebrate your Scorpio pals today!

INVITATION

Reach out to your Scorpio pals to tell them you love them and why!

Encouragement

Today, I want to whisper these words to you: "Don't be so hard on yourself, love. We cannot thrive in a world of should and not enough. You are navigating a full and complicated life. You ask a lot of yourself every single day. Walk forward gently. Do not tear yourself apart for what you have yet to become. Find peace in small victories or accomplishments. You do not have to hide what you feel is imperfect or awkward. We are all imperfect and awkward. We are all fragile and irrepressibly strong. We are walking paradoxes, and that's OK. Do not feel you have to be only one way—brave, strong, invincible. Embrace the messiest parts of yourself and let them see the light of day. Stop sometimes and lay your burden down. Do nothing. Listen, breathe, wonder. Please do not speak to yourself harshly. Be a friend to your loving self."

INVITATION

Whisper the above to yourself. Read it slowly. Take it in.

Scorpio

Investing

Scorpio is one of the great financial signs. Simply put, it knows something about money, resources, and manifesting. Even if we are still working on the financial realm of our lives, let's think about what we would do with more financial resources. Where would we invest? What do we believe in? What do we want to help manifest? What are we called to create? Scorpio is passionate and wants to work powerfully in the world, and organizing our finances can help facilitate powerful action.

INVITATION

Practice investing in the name of what you value. As an experiment, you might set up a way to invest even a small amount of money each week ($5!) and dedicate it to something meaningful for you. It may be that you are seeding a trip or a home or a car. Or maybe you want to invest in the name of a charity you love and believe in. Watch your investment grow slowly and fruitfully over time.

I Wonder

Let's start quietly and ease our way into the day. Let's forgive ourselves five times before we even get out of bed. Let's breathe to release what we need not carry. Let's light the lantern of our hearts and recognize that we are strong and can expose and transform any shadows. Let's investigate what is causing us pain, turn it over in our gentle palm, in our loving mind, and see if we can find kindness or resolution, any relief for this day. Let us see if we can let past resentment or irritation dissolve in the love a new day offers. Let us stay open and curious about this new day.

INVITATION

Curiosity heals many ills. If strong feelings come up for you today, use this phrase: "I wonder . . ." You could say, "I wonder why I suddenly feel this way?" Or, "I wonder if there is anything I could do that would make me feel slightly better?" Or, "I wonder if there is anything about this feeling that could be helpful?" Practice holding your feelings with curiosity.

Scorpio

Praise Song

Praise song for Scorpio. You are the deepest mystery, a wielder of power, a well of feeling. Praise song for Scorpio. You who face your fears. You who are searingly honest. You who are passionate and rise above the pain. Praise song for Scorpio. Keeper of secrets, warrior hearts. We can all live in these potent waters today. We can overcome pain, fear or adversity. Today, we can be brave. Today, we can do hard things. Praise song for Scorpio.

INVITATION

Today, write a praise song or poem for any sign you choose! Celebrate the energies with which you are working. Read it out loud to a friend.

Humor

Humor is necessary. Humor heals! If tired or challenged, search for humor. Scorpios often have a great dark sense of humor. And that actually helps. It's intense work to wrestle our fears into the light of day, but it doesn't have to be joyless. Dig deep, shed skins, and laugh hard. That actually sounds like a strangely perfect day. Don't let fear win.

INVITATION

Find some go-to podcasts that just speak to your soul. Find people who allow you to belly-laugh. Watch stand-up comedy. Give yourself to the replenishment of laughter.

Scorpio

Catharsis

The Merriam-Webster definition of *catharsis* is: 1. "purification or purgation of the emotions (such as pity and fear) primarily through art. 2. "a purification or purgation that brings about spiritual renewal or release from tension." I love that this spiritual renewal and release could happen primarily through art. And I think this definition is a beautiful invitation to us all to dance, write, sing, sculpt, paint, act, weave through and into what we feel to name it and know it, and then release it. Scorpio is ultimately a time to heal and strengthen. And sometimes we do so by walking the burning ground. We invite catharsis and ultimately metamorphosis through whatever artistic medium we choose. Our artistic offering calls in the gods of transformation.

INVITATION

Our willingness to move, write, play, and create says, "Yes, I am ready to heal." Let your inner artist out today. Make something. Anything. Don't judge it. Let it work on you.

The Eagle and the Scorpion

The scorpion and the eagle are both deeply connected with Scorpio. The less evolved Scorpio energy is that of the scorpion. It can be brutal and destructive, defensive and out to kill. As we grow more skilled and loving using the energy of Scorpio, the eagle becomes more significant. The eagle flies above the emotional landscape. It surveys the situation. It knows its power, but chooses wisely when and how to use it. The eagle represents power and self-control. Humanity is particularly working out the energies of Scorpio. How do we each choose wisely in areas concerning sex or money, or when we feel fear, hatred, pride, or ambition? We evolve as we make each choice. The evolved Scorpio is the phoenix. It rises from the ashes of its old self and moves forward in the world to heal and lead. The phoenix is transformed. We are all transformed under Scorpio if we practice patience, truth-telling, right use of power, and self-control.

INVITATION

Let's write: "Today, I choose . . . "

Sit with It

Get quiet. Breathe. Follow the feeling that presents itself. Follow it and name it and sit with it. Don't lash out. Don't attack. Don't try to kill it or anyone who happens to cross your path. Sit with it. Name it. Don't be fixed about how you will heal it. Others have felt and will feel as intensely as you do. Others have wrestled their way into the light and will do so again. Now it's your turn. Do so humbly. Surrender your sword. Feel the fear and pain that wants to govern you. Refuse. Soften. Refuse again. Soften again. Feel compassion for your struggling self. Open yourself to some-thing greater and more vast than yourself. Feel a rain of love and grace forever falling on you. Hold your pain and fear close to your heart. Then offer it to light. Repeat with tenderness, humility, and self-compassion.

INVITATION

Let today be the day that those three words—tenderness, humility, and self-compassion—accompany you throughout your day. Say them out loud. Can you do everything you need to do today and still embody those words? Is there anything you can do today to amplify those qualities in your life?

Dear Scorpio

Oh, Scorpio. You're intense, deep, sexy, and a badass. You are the warrior queen. You are the warrior king. You let it rip. You don't hold back. You inspire with your fierce truth-telling. But to be fair, it's easy to feel a little nervous when you approach. You tend to rock worlds in one way or another. You help us feel strong, tenacious, rich, and unstoppable, or send us to the depths of our wretched struggle. Beloved Scorpio, help us all show up in our days with a willingness to do the work—whether that's emotional, mental, or physical. We are willing to change, grow, shed, trans- form. Just try not to push too many of our buttons all at once, because then we'll probably get reactive. Let's proceed together with strength and prudence. Let's do the healing work that lets us feel a little lighter. Let's write, move, investigate. Let's fiercely commit to well-being, creativity, and growth.

INVITATION

Lie down on your bed or a yoga mat and completely surrender. Let go. Scorpio does not love to loosen its grip, but make yourself avail- able to accept whatever comes your way. There is no need to control a thing today. Feel your power even in this completely surrendered state.

Symbols

Let's look at the symbol for Scorpio. Let's think about the movement of creating it. The pen goes down, up, down, up, down, and
then culminates with an upward shooting arrow. Is it the sting
of the scorpion or directed power for the good? Scorpio always
offers us an emotional ride, and it's often an extreme one. It's
important to remember the depths when we are high and the
highs when we are low. It's also important to remember there
is a middle ground. Scorpio will feel better when it remembers
that nothing is fixed. When in Scorpio, we are always sure we will
be angry, sad, elated forever. Our work is to remind ourselves,
moment to moment, that we are forever, however imperceptibly
and with a few confused turns, growing toward the light.

INVITATION

I invite you to simply draw the symbol for Scorpio. Draw it quickly.
Draw it slowly. Make a big Scorpio splash and then hide it in the corner of the page. See how it feels to trace the lines of Scorpio.

Meeting Our Gaze

Let's fall in love with the night, with the soft darkness as it cloaks the day, with the great silences that speak. Let us fall in love with the hard truth and the fierce gaze, the loyal friend and the worthy foe. Let us not run from the struggle but stand true and weather the storm. Let us fall in love with any weariness that leads us to open a new door, any letting go that welcomes new life. Let us learn to love our hidden shame and our frightened not-enoughness. Let us rock our own mortality in our loving arms and soothe our fears of what we cannot know. Let us meet our own gaze in the mirror without judgment—curious and willing.

INVITATION

Meet your own gaze in the mirror without judgment. Stay there for a time. Befriend yourself.

Scorpio

Naming Fear

Today, let's name a great fear. Let's say it out loud. Say it again. Then let's take the deepest breath we've taken in a long time. And another. Let's soften our brows. Let's stop trying to hide or ignore the fear. Let's feel palpable light all around us. Let's practice releasing that fear to dissolve into something greater and vaster than ourselves. With each exhale, let it dissolve further. Then let's name how we would like to flourish in our lives. Let's say it out loud. Do we want to fall in love? Release a pattern that doesn't serve us? Be acknowledged for what we do? Breathe. Feel our own spine and our heart. Let's stand and trust and be open to possibility.

INVITATION

Name your fear.

Say it out loud.

Take a deep breath.

Soften.

Name how you'd like to flourish.

Breathe.

Trust.

Open yourself to the possibility.

Moving a Mood

A mood is just a feeling we've chosen to hold on to and amplify. When we hold onto a mood, we brood. We sit in the thick of pain. Today, practice noticing and letting go, noticing and letting go. Practice softening the mood in the privacy of your own home, where others will not be affected; amplify and exaggerate your mood. And then, yes, let it go. Let it flow through. Invite it in and usher it out. Make something, write something, dance it, shake it, speak it. Don't sit in it.

INVITATION

Now, ask yourself what kind of Scorpio day you'd like to have: Strong? Sexy? Secretive? Surrendered? Deep? Dark? Delicious? Tenacious? Triumphant? Intense? Investigative? Set an intention for the day. How will you use this powerful, potent, healing, transformative Scorpio magic today?

Scorpio

Pitch-Black

Imagine pitch-black. Imagine the kind of darkness that is so dark it's as if your eyes are closed. And then remember how always in that kind of darkness, if you wait, breathe, and adjust, eventually the dark reveals a shape, a texture, a sound. Eventually we are able to orient ourselves a fraction more than moments before. The key is not to panic or react in fear. The key is to stop, breathe, listen, and look for clues. This is exactly what we need to do whenever we feel pitch black within. First, we have to sit and be open to the intensity of the dark, but then we must be willing for it to touch us. We have to feel it as familiar. We listen. We don't collapse. Then we begin to see what is hidden within it. Shapes begin to appear as messengers offering direction. There may be whispers, invitations, needs that must be heard. The depths are the realm of growth and truth-telling. The secrets of ourselves eventually open to greater light. When in Scorpio, stay calm, listen, walk calmly forward. The mysteries of the dark fuel and strengthen us.

INVITATION

Find a time tonight to sit or stand in the dark, whether indoors or outdoors. See how dark you can make it, and then let the dark start to whisper to you. Allow yourself to soften to receive its gifts.

Crashing Satellites

Scorpio insists that we feel it all. It reminds us that it is necessary and relieving to acknowledge the pain. I read a headline recently about two satellites possibly crashing in the atmosphere. And I kid you not, the headline read, "This is really, really bad news." I laughed. There is something refreshing about a news headline naming the intensity as it is. Underlying stress and unnamed fear leave us very wobbly. Let's make sure we talk about it. There's something about saying, "I'm really feeling wretched" that helps us begin to shift. Likewise, "I'm really feeling a bit more hopeful." Hopeful creates a touchstone from which we can build.

INVITATION

Let's write: "This is really, really bad news." Then, if you feel like it: "I feel hopeful about . . ."

Sagittarius Is Knocking

We are at a threshold time. Scorpio is offering its last whispers before Sagittarius, the sign of fiery focus, takes center stage. Scorpio gives us one last chance to shed or release the old. It reminds us that we are in the process of becoming and we are not beholden to any earlier version of ourselves. The shedding, the breaking free, the cracking open, the surrender. We are making space for a new self, one we cannot now fully imagine. Sagittarius will help us look to the new horizon. It will offer a new dream. Today, we can surrender just a bit more in preparation for fiery renewal.

INVITATION

Let's write: "I no longer need to carry." Go for 15 minutes. Read your answer out loud to a friend.

Sagittarius

Welcoming Sagittarius

Today, we welcome the encouragement, optimism, and vision of Sagittarius. We enter the month of adventure, risk taking, education, and a broadened perspective. This is one of the great signs of freedom. This month, we dream big and then we dare ourselves to go on a great quest in pursuit of that dream. We work toward increasing levels of freedom, within and without. Education plays a big role in this third of the three fire signs (Aries, Leo and Sagittarius). We teach and we educate ourselves. We inspire. We mentor. We uplift. And we move. Sagittarius rules the legs, carrying us forward with great momentum. What do we envision for the month ahead?

INVITATION

Sagittarius is ever naming its next horizon. Today, begin to articulate your next goal, big or small. Be sure to celebrate when you arrive.

Travel

In *The Innocents Abroad*, Mark Twain wrote, "Travel is fatal to prejudice, bigotry, and narrow-mindedness, and many of our people need it sorely on these accounts. Broad, wholesome, charitable views of men and things cannot be acquired by vegetating in one little corner of the earth all one's lifetime." Sagittarius invites us to travel to distant lands and outside our comfort zones. It longs for growth, new horizons, and unexpected adventures. When in Sagittarius, it's an opportunity to say yes to something new, untried, yet to be explored. It's a day to plan our next big trip.

INVITATION

If you can't make a big out-in-the-world trip, take an inner adventure. Read books by authors very different from yourself. Explore other countries through the page. Expand your horizons. Learn to say, "I love you" in three new languages!

Sagittarius

Imagine This

Today, imagine this: You are on a beautiful horse and you are galloping across an open field. You feel free. You can hear your own breathing. You can hear the horse's hooves. It is waking up everything inside you. You are tasting freedom. You are tasting adventure. You are riding fast enough that it feels like a thrill and a risk. You are being carried. You feel light, and the space around you is suffused with possibility. Today, you say yes. Yesterday, you could not. But today you choose yes. You are no longer tired. You do not feel burdened. You are as the wind. Remember this, you think. Then you laugh. No, just love this. Now today, sweet fellow riders, close your eyes and ride. Energy follows thought. Your body and your breath will catch the scent of this expanse and will carry you someplace new.

INVITATION

Today, just watch horses run, in person or online. Feel the power and possibility. Breathe it in.

Visionary

The Oxford English Dictionary defines visionary as: "thinking about or planning the future with imagination or wisdom." And also, "a person with original ideas about what the future will or could be like." Sagittarius is the sign of the visionary. And today we can all experiment with being the visionary of our own lives. The key seems to be thinking about the future with imagination, letting ourselves have original ideas about our original lives. Wisdom is the marriage of the head and the heart. And when we look forward with both, for our individual selves and our communities and our country, then things start to get exciting. Let's dare ourselves to see what is truly possible.

INVITATION

Spend some time in nature looking to the farthest horizon you can see. Let yourself think about a few big dreams you have for your life. Breathe in the horizon and breathe in the dream.

Sagittarius

The Earth

Sagittarius is the sign of the planetary citizen. It loves to explore the planet Earth—all the countries, peoples, and species around the globe. It is motivated to speak for and protect this planet, to celebrate it with awe and wonder. Many Sagittarians are drawn to work in the world of climate change, animal preservation, or more sustainable living. As Sagittarius evolves, its focus becomes less about the next adventure and more about how its particular focus and dedication can benefit humanity and the planet.

INVITATION

To incite a little awe, wonder, and deep appreciation for our planet, watch the television programs *Planet Earth* or *The Blue Planet*. Feel the inspiration of being introduced to all the many species around our globe. Feel the splendor and beauty of the planet itself.

Our Inner Cheerleader

Under Sagittarius, our own inner cheerleader comes out to play. We encourage our weary selves and say, "We can do this! This is possible. We're doing a good job." All we have to do is actually *welcome* our inner cheerleader instead of sending her away with our lethargy or doubt. What does our inner cheerleader want to say to us? What message of hope does that inner voice bring? It's OK to bet on ourselves. It's more than OK to believe fully in our potential and to carry possibility in our pockets. When in Sagittarius, we can expand our vision for ourselves. We can summon our inner and outer strength and feel our freedom. We can take off, set sail with our inner cheerleader at our side.

INVITATION

Write a letter to yourself as if from your most loving self. Celebrate your life at this moment, even if you are navigating a difficult hour. Celebrate *how* you are navigating that difficult hour. Use your own words to cheer yourself on.

Sagittarius

World Friendship

At the back of the Kresge auditorium at Interlochen Center for the Arts in Michigan are these words: "Dedicated to the promotion of world friendship through the universal language of the arts." Sagittarius loves holding a big dream with tremendous optimism. Sagittarius says, "World friendship is possible." Sagittarius says, "Hold your vision. Keep the faith. Do not despair. It says, "We are world citizens. We must encourage our mutual growth." On a Sagittarius day, let's look forward and channel our power and focus for the good. We can think of our friends and allies across the globe.

INVITATION

Do you have friends across the globe? Wouldn't it be wonderful if we thought of ourselves as global citizens? How would we tend to the planet and treat one another if we thought of ourselves in that way? Today, reach out to one of your global friends.

The Unknown

We yearn to learn, grow, and travel beyond our known landscape. We search for deeper truths as we head for new horizons. We have to get out of our own comfort zones. Sagittarius is a sign that supports taking a risk. It lives and breathes for the unknown. Every Sagittarius day needs some sort of quest or self-discovery. Remember that Sagittarius rules higher education and that education is one of the best ways to live into the unknown and grow our understanding of the world.

INVITATION

What language would you like to become more fluent in? Learn a few words in that language today. Or, what religion do you know very little about? Read a bit about it, and its main tenets, today. Be willing to expand your understanding of the world by learning more about it.

Sagittarius

Our Teachers

Let's think of one of our favorite mentors or teachers. How do we feel in their presence? What do they bring forth in us? How are we changed for having met them? Now and then, and always, it's beautiful to stop and remember how we got to this moment and who guided, motivated, or encouraged us to our next horizon. Teachers open our minds and blast open our hearts, helping us extend beyond old self-definitions, inviting us to deepen our understanding of self in the world. Every great teacher helps us move out of limited beliefs or stuck places and opens us to renewed vision. What teachers changed your life? What would we do without our teachers? Who has changed your life forever just by their willingness to offer their gift?

INVITATION

What can you do today to honor your teachers? What can you do to affirm and grow what you have been taught? How can you thank those who have gifted you with their love and wisdom through your actions?

Our Sagittarius Friends

Here are all the reasons it's good to have a Sagittarius friend:

1. They will inspire you to take risks and say yes to your life.

2. They will invite you to travel with them to many exotic locations.

3. They are buoyant, optimistic, and forward-thinking.

4. They will be your ultimate cheerleader.

5. They love to run and jump and be frisky. And sometimes that's really fun.

6. They love to grow. They love their teachers and they love to teach.

7. They will happily play *truth or dare* with you and tell all the truths and dare all the dares.

8. They will tell you what they think.

9. They always truly do believe that everything is going to be OK. And they will always help you believe it too.

Let's celebrate our Sagittarius pals!

INVITATION

Let's reach out to our Sagittarius pals to tell them we love them and why!

Yes

Sagittarius rules the quest! It envisions the new. We are buoyed and feel that whatever it is we see as our next step, we can do it. The planet Jupiter rules Sagittarius. It offers the blessing of yes. Yes, we can. Yes, it's possible. Yes, things will improve. Yes, give it a try. We grow because we dare ourselves to be more than we are. We grow because we take a risk. We grow because we envision a fuller expression for ourselves. No one gives up under Sagittarius. So apply for that grant. Buy the ticket to Ireland. Go back to school. Grow.

INVITATION

It's a day to take a risk, make the call, write the email, jump in the ocean, tell your person you love them for the first time. Move your body in a new way. Tell someone the truth. Finally decide to quit your job. Sing in the grocery store. Expand, bust out, decide to go back to school. Book a flight to Paris. Say yes.

Use Your Words

Take 5 minutes now and write yourself an encouraging sentence using any of the following very Sagittarius words. Then share your inspiration with someone—a friend, a love, an ally. Here are the words: aim, discover, inspire, chase, chance, quest, adventure, seek, buoyant, risk, motivate, gamble, journey, travel, mission, goal, free, freedom, reckless, growth, grow, more, abundance, reach, path, target, uplift, search, pilgrimage, arouse, envision. At the very least, read all those words aloud or use one in a sentence.

INVITATION

Here's one possibility: "I am wild and free, inspired to set off on a quest for growth and inspiration." Try a few. You'll feel Sagittarius in your body the moment you speak the words aloud.

Sagittarius

Arrows

Let's feel the fiery gift of Sagittarius burning through our heaviness, lighting a new way. Let's exercise our bodies and our spirits. This momentum and movement of Sagittarius motivates us to outgrow our current thoughts or definition of self. It reminds us to dream of the possible and not always resign ourselves to the probable. It invites us to be archers aiming for our true target. Tell me what's one small goal you have for this day. Now pull an arrow from your quiver, place it in your bow, steady your aim, and let loose. Stay clear and focused. You're on your way.

INVITATION

Give yourself one tiny, clear focus for the day. Once that goal is achieved, celebrate it. And then, if you like, draw another arrow from your quiver.

Willingness

Adventures require flexibility. Growth requires willingness and adaptability; if we head off on a Sagittarian quest, we will be surprised along the way. The very nature of adventure involves relinquishing control. We invite the new, the startling, the unexpected. We invite the awkwardness of growth. We allow ourselves to wobble and make our way through uncharted territory. Risk requires surrender. We surrender the part of ourselves that protects the ego at all costs. We render ourselves willing and raw and we try to experience the world through new eyes. Sagittarius invites us to look ahead and feel what is possible and then encourages us to say yes, even as it starts to feel a little scary or unpredictable. Sagittarius says, "You are walking on new ground."

INVITATION

Let's write. Every great adventure involves risk. Use this prompt and see where it takes you: "I am willing to risk it."

Sagittarius

Louise

Freedom is Sagittarius's middle name. When in Sagittarius, we tire of old constraints. We tire of old rhythms and patterns. We want to break free and grow. If you haven't read the children's book by Kate DiCamilo, *Louise, The Adventures of a Chicken*, do so. Louise, a chicken, leaves her henhouse and sails the seas with pirates. She joins the circus. She's even kidnapped. Eventually she returns to her home sweet home and tells the stories of her adventures. Sagittarius is the storyteller and inspires us all with all it has seen and experienced. So today let some fresh air fill our lungs and remember what vitality and daring feel like.

INVITATION

What has been your greatest adventure to date? Why? What made it adventurous? What are the ingredients of adventure? What did you learn? How did you grow? Tell a friend and ask them about one of theirs.

New Visions

This is an excerpt of my poem "Freedom Yet to Find."

What is known is always knocking.
You do not have to answer.
Fling open the back door
To the YES of unspeakable light
And boundless time.

The invitation ever exists—
If there is a hint,
Whiff, touch,
Whisper of freedom
Left to find,

Ready your ship.
Let the winds blow.
Refuse the map of discovered worlds.
Let love be your compass.
Set sail.

INVITATION

Read the poem above slowly and out loud. (Remember, the full version is available at www.heidirose.com/poetry.)

Stories

Once upon a time, five women sat around a table. One was grieving the death of her mother, one had never felt so nervous and jangly inside, one had job and financial worries, another was deep in the turbulent waters of a painful break up, and one did not know whether she would have the child she wanted to have. They shared stories and cried many tears. They lit candles and ate good food. And at one point, they laughed so hard and so long, they could barely ride the release. When they said goodbye, every one of them went home feeling lighter, relieved for tears, laughter, storytelling, and good company. Sagittarius carries hope and renewal and new visions of all that may come to be. May we carry this fire inside today.

INVITATION

Gather friends and tell stories. Ask a question that all in the circle answer. Listen deeply. Hold one another in the storytelling.

Beacons

Can we see it? Can we name it? Then we can begin to move toward it. So much depends on the ability to see a little light ahead. That's all. We need a lighthouse of sorts to signal us from our own future. "Walk this way, love. Here is a safe harbor. You've come this far. Onward. Don't give up. Here is solid ground." Let's move toward that beacon, that light. Let's feel a hand at our back. And sometimes we can be that beacon, that lighthouse, that hand at the back, for another.

INVITATION

Remember, one lighthouse provides the light to reach the next. We move from light to light. Navigate your day like this today—light to light to light.

Sagittarius

The Journey You've Yet to Take

Every time my mom travels, she listens to the song from Don Quixote "To Dream the Impossible Dream" on the way to the airport. She loves to be taking off on a new adventure. She loves the possibility. What is a journey you have yet to take? It can be an inner or outer journey, a journey of liberation or dedication. It can be a journey across the seas or into your very heart. Is it a new longing or one you have carried for years? Sagittarius asks us to name the journeys we've yet to take and in so doing, inspire ourselves and one another.

INVITATION

Sometimes, creating a vision board or a collage helps us dream or clarify our longing. Visit an art store and gather what you need to collage your way into your next journey.

Making Room

Here are two stanzas from my poem "The Quivering":

If we but soften our grasp
On who we have always been,
To make room for what can be
Knowing not what may appear,
Knowing only
the quivering,

And I ask,
Is not some part of us always dying?
And I ask,
Are we not everyday
In some small way
Reborn?

INVITATION

Here is your writing prompt: "Making room for what can be."

Sagittarius

A Good Day

What makes a good day? What are the small things that lift our spirits, that bring hope or presence or love? It's easy to feel the too muchness of our times. We can't always be heroic in big ways, but we can be heroic in shaping our lives to hold more light. It just takes practice. So I ask again, what makes a good day? How can we make a difficult day better? Here are a few possible ingredients:

1. Solitude—a kind of deep listening and receiving

2. Beauty—acknowledging something beautiful

3. Connection—a call, a touch, a check-in, helping another

4. A good meal for ourselves or another

5. Writing—what you really feel

6. An act of kindness or a selfless act; it always sets us straight

7. Creativity—writing a poem, sketching, baking, singing

8. Follow inspiration—a good book, a podcast, music

9. Movement—a walk, a class, an impromptu dance

10. Breathing—ever and always, deep, beautiful breaths

INVITATION

Just one of these will grow the light and goodness of our day. Choose one. Invite a friend to choose one as well. Make it a good day for yourself and another.

Out of Doors

Have you ever noticed how deeply calming it is to gaze at the horizon? It offers perspective and hope. It's important when we feel most stuck or sad to get out of doors where we can see something far away, even if it's just the sky meeting a distant hill. We all need perspective. Let's notice the dance of life all around us and how there is always a horizon in the distance that promises something new. And sometimes the best way to lift our spirits is to actually move with momentum, over distance, and toward that horizon.

INVITATION

Today, your task is simple: Get outside! Choose something to move toward. Run or briskly walk there. Choose another destination and do the same. Then, look to the horizon and breathe it in.

Sagittarius

Our Legs

Sagittarius rules our legs! It rules skiing, running, and leaping. If you want to get the simplest taste of the Sagittarius energy, just try a sprint! Engage the power of the greatest muscles in your body. Run like the wind. And if that's not in the cards, you can lean toward the philosophical resonances of Sagittarius. It can be a mental sprint instead, a quest to understand.

INVITATION

When I am feeling most lethargic or depressed, sometimes I just boot myself out the door to sprint! I'm not a runner, but even running for 1 to 2 minutes shifts something internally. If you are able, make today a sprint day!

Tiny Steps

Let's celebrate small victories. No, really. Life isn't often an ongoing stream of huge growth spurts. We have to pay attention to the tiny steps. Every tiny step is still growth. Grace presents itself when we even begin to lean in the right direction. So, notice the incremental growth. Note when we feel just a little lighter than yesterday. Some days we may not feel like getting out of bed. Growth (and a tiny victory) may look like getting up and sitting on the couch for ten minutes with a cup of tea and not immediately requiring anything of ourselves. Growth may look like a walk around the block. Let's give ourselves time to get where we are going and treat ourselves like we matter.

INVITATION

Make a list of your small victories of this past week. Don't dismiss anything as too small. Make sure to read it through and let each small victory really land in you. It might be as simple as "Yesterday when I woke up, I opened the back door and took three deep breaths. It felt good."

Sagittarius

Recover

Today, let's take a breath and recover. We all have something large or small from which we need to regroup, recover, or replenish. The solution is not always to press onward. We can feel glimmers of hope without leaping to action. Sometimes we need digestion time, assimilation time. Today, let's not act if we don't want to or don't feel ready. We don't even have to summon positivity. Let's just be with what is and soften. Let's be curious about how our lives are unfolding. Let's trust the timing. Our worlds are being rocked repeatedly these days, and honestly we have to allow for more room to breathe, express, and rest.

INVITATION

Lie down for 5 minutes sometime today. Just stop. Feel your body supported by your bed or by the earth. Let yourself exhale any unnecessary tension. Give it to what lies beneath you. Completely rest. Put your hand on your brow and smooth away the activity of your mind. Completely stop.

Foresee Fulfillment

Foresee fulfillment. These two words are instructive and full of possibility. It is far too easy to stay focused on all that feels not enough. We make lists of everything broken, insufficient, or lacking. We can easily dwell in the land of our faults. We create entire stories about how we, the heroes and heroines of our own stories, probably won't find absolute joyous success. But what if we foresee fulfillment as a practice? What if we breathe beyond feelings of insufficiency and, instead, envision and embody momentum and growth? What if we invite grace on our forward moving journey? What if we invite patience and trust? Let us foresee our fulfillment, my friends. Know it will be so. And while we're at it, let's foresee fulfillment for those we love. And even those we don't love. No one else's true soul fulfillment will ever impede another's. We are each to thrive.

INVITATION

Choose three people in your life and take a few moments with each to imagine one possible, beautiful unfolding of their lives. Hold the vision of their growth and blossoming. Bless their ever unfurling path. Energy follows thought. With every tiny bit of blessing and encouragement, even from afar, we buoy one another.

Sagittarius

Maps

Remember the old maps in your third-grade classroom? Remember looking at an entirely different continent and wondering if you'd ever visit it? Remember all the ocean? Sagittarius sees a map and is ready to go. She spins the globe, closes her eyes, points, and buys her plane ticket. Maps are inspiring because it means there's more world to explore. And when we explore more of the world, we grow more compassionate and wise. We grow inwardly and we explore outwardly.

INVITATION

Buy a map of a place you'd like to visit. Or, buy a world map and push pins in all the places you'd like to eventually see! Look at this map often. Even just looking at a map reminds us of how vast and how full of possibility this world is.

Yours to Tell

Tell me the story that is yours to tell. Tell me your story of this moment in your life. I might say, "I am in the thick of my life, curious and hugely grateful, but also navigating lots of sadness." I might also say, "I talked with Dad early yesterday morning and I cried telling him about a movie I had just watched and loved. And he lives an ocean away." Or "All I want to do is write. I want to write poems and promises and love notes and essays. I want to write myself into a greater freedom." Tell your story, tell me a story that is just yours to tell at this moment.

INVITATION

Call a friend. Read them your story, your words, your self-discovery. Sharing stories is balm. Let's be a balm for one another.

Sagittarius

Rhythm of the Signs

Can you feel the rhythm of the shift of signs from positive to negative polarity and back again? There is expansion and contraction or outward versus inner action. Aries comes forth. Taurus magnetizes. Gemini connects. Cancer nourishes and protects. Leo expresses. Virgo refines. Libra comes forth in the name of relationship. Scorpio wrestles and heals. Sagittarius explores. Capricorn quietly climbs. Aquarius shares. Pisces imagines and loves. As we approach the shift into this new sign, let's feel the shift from the fire of Sagittarius to the earth of Capricorn. Let's feel the shift from adventure to purpose. Our quest to the mountain is ending and now the mountain is before us. The silence of the summit beckons.

INVITATION

Today, simply notice that you are in a time of transition. You are beginning to turn inward, even as the world seems to get busier. You begin to quiet within. Something clear, quiet, and calm enters. Listen.

Capricorn

Welcoming Capricorn

Today, we welcome Capricorn. Capricorn scales from the darkest depths to the most luminous heights. Each of us must make the pilgrimage to the mountaintop of our lives, guided by the light within and the light we each carry. There will be times as we climb that we are very much alone with only our little light to guide the way. And there are times when we reach vistas and see hundreds, thousands of us climbing, breathing, treading the path. Capricorn (and its ruler Saturn) also rule time. During this month, we work to use time well. We work to be on time for ourselves and others. The bottom line about this month is that Capricorn is indeed a sign of great ambition, striving, effort, and commitment. It is a sign that takes life very seriously and feels responsible for everything and everyone. It's a powerful month to commit. But, exertion without heart can be ruthless or exhausting. Striving without rest is debilitating. The key is to use these first weeks of Capricorn to come to know our quiet power within, to carve out room for silence. Then, in the New Year, we emerge replenished and ready, lit from within, and carrying a light for others. Travel well. Travel in love. The summit is only a moment at the end of an extraordinary journey.

INVITATION

Breathe in resolve. Breathe in this solstice moment when the light, again, begins to grow. May it be so within and without.

Clear Steps

Capricorn can offer such exquisite gifts. No matter the hardship and in great times of grief or pain, Capricorn continues. It supports and steadies all that is tender and vulnerable. It sees us through. Capricorn keeps it together and creates a plan amid the chaos. It takes clear steps, offering solidity and great practical care. Amid pain, it soothes through concrete action. Capricorn is capable of offering great parental wisdom and kindness. It is willing to be in charge and take care of those who need the greatest care today. Let us feel our own inner Capricorn. Let us feel the wise, strong place within. Today, feel the relief of structure. Let us be our own kind parent and feel our steadiness and strength.

INVITATION

Sometimes, the simplest adjustment in your body shifts your inner life. If possible, I invite you to sit upright and to feel the great gift of your spine. Feel its structure and support. Feel how your uprightness helps evoke purpose. If you are unable to sit upright, imagine the energy of your spine holding you.

Capricorn

Time

Capricorn rules time. We each have to ask ourselves if we need a *stronger* relationship with concrete time, or perhaps a kinder, looser relationship with its pressure and severity. Capricorn offers the practice of punctuality and right timing. For those who tend to live in a dreamy way, it supports with structure and accountability. But there are some of us who have too intense a relationship with time and time pressure, and actually need to back off from the sense that we're out of time or running out of time, or we're late, late, late. Capricorn asks us to create a healthy relationship with time. Do we need clear deadlines and time frames or might we benefit from a deeper trust, letting all unfold with an ever-increasing ease?

INVITATION

If you are a person who loves your watch or the clock on your phone, try to go without that today. See how it feels to walk through the day without a constant reference to outside time. Or, if you feel you live most of your life like that already, try doing the exact opposite. Do you have a watch you could wear for a day? What does it feel to have time walking with you?

Lay Aside Doubt

Capricorn says, "You've got this. You've been growing steadily until this very day. And you've learned a few things. It is time to lay aside doubt and breathe in your own authority." Capricorn says, "Feel the earth beneath your feet. Set off. Feel your upright-ness and your steadiness." Capricorn might also tickle you now and then, and say, "Why so serious, buckaroo? This life is filled with pleasure. Yes, do your work. But don't forget to play." There's a moment in life when we realize we get to be our own loving parent. We can tend to our own well-being with exquisite care and attention. We can choose to nourish ourselves. Let's leave those punitive voices behind. Let's whisper encouragement in our own ears, remembering who we truly are. It's a beautiful day to set ourselves right and begin again.

INVITATION

The next time you hop in the shower, give yourself a pep talk! No one is going to hear and the water washes away all the negative self-talk. Every shower is a fresh start.

Capricorn

What Love Brings

Today, my friends, I wish us deep inner quiet—the kind of quiet that allows something new to be born or transform within us. I wish us the opportunity to feel the depth of our own love and to find ourselves sharing it across time and distance. I wish us forgiveness and perspective and renewal. I wish for us a day of the deepest joy. Let there be music in the house. I wish for us to climb under the layer of chaos and find a stillness that is like a river of unceasing love. I send you great love on this day. Drink it in if you feel alone. Drink it in regardless.

INVITATION

Let's write: "Love says . . ."

Wise Use of Slow Action

Capricorn offers us the wise use of slow action. Capricorn rules time and reminds us everything is slowly and steadily evolving. Use Capricorn to calmly do what next needs to be done. Use Capricorn to build wisely and sturdily. Be full of care and deeply attentive.

INVITATION

Today, let's work with the qualities of patience and pace. Simply ask yourself: what is the next right thing to do? Slow your pace and trust patiently that all is unfolding in the right timing. Keep your eye on the prize, but refuse to rush to get there.

Capricorn

Silence

It's good to be truly silent with ourselves now and then. So often the inner critical, worried voices take up too much room. How can we listen beyond the inner and outer chatter? How can we listen at a deeper level? True silence is imbued with love and aliveness. And often the way into the richest silence is through the breath or a long, luxurious walk. Movement and breath are portals into rich silence. We can begin even now.

INVITATION

After reading this, put down the book. Feel your feet on the earth. Close your eyes and breathe. Listen beyond the sounds in the room. Listen further out. Hear the birdsong or the rush of traffic. Then, listen further still. If you have time and the inclination, take yourself out on a listening walk.

No Need to Go It Alone

Capricorn rules commitment and determination. Once we've said yes, Capricorn is the energy that sees us through. It walks steadily and doesn't expend extra effort. Capricorn says, "I have the patience necessary to see commitments come to fruition." But here's the thing: We don't have to do it alone. We don't have to feel lonely on our journey. We can value the group and value our community. We can ask our friends and allies to witness our commitment and our next line of growth. We can ask them to hold us accountable and cheer us on.

INVITATION

This is our reminder that commitment does not mean isolation. We do not have to disappear into our intensity just because we want to see something through. We need the support of our allies. Whatever plan you have, let a few friends in on the journey. Today, talk with a friend about something you are wanting to accomplish and ask them to witness your journey and encourage you along the way.

Capricorn

Putting Our Burdens Down

You don't have to work on your life every day. You don't have to strive to be better every day. You don't have to put your best forward or improve yourself every day. No, my sweet friends, some days are for putting our burdens down. Some days are a song to be sung. A walk in the woods. A hammock nap. Some days are for no one and nothing but your own self and your trusty inner compass. Life does not have to be one great climb. It can be a swim across the lake, baking fresh bread, communing with a tree that is also a friend. We are not meant to always be tired, stretched to the limit or at empty. Perhaps we find fullness by not filling every moment. I wish you a solid day of spaciousness and ease, tender steps and rest today. Today, live your life and don't worry about fixing it.

INVITATION

Today, put away any to-do list. Start today with ease and curiosity and as much room for pleasure as possible.

Stay Home

Sometimes Capricorn just needs to stay home and expand the idea of what hearth and home means. Home can be hearth, home base, the center point, the still point, family or protection. When we stay home, we can think of it as an invitation to stay close to the truth, core, and heartbeat of who we are. When we stay home, we can listen, stay quiet, and receive. Let us stay home in the seat of our own nourishment. Let us stay home in the seat of mother love. Let's take this time to build our houses of light with love, courage, and calm. Let's stay home and come home to ourselves.

INVITATION

Yes, work calls, and many of us can't actually "stay home." But let us keep coming home to the center of ourselves. Sometimes, just placing a hand on our heart is all the homecoming we need.

Capricorn

Sparkler

Sometimes we need to light a sparkler. It's so easy to get very, very serious when we are in Capricorn and it's important to remember that we all need big heaping amounts of joy too. It's actually sparkly and gorgeous to feel purposeful and to be pursuing our goals. But it's also enormously important to remember to play and laugh and be spontaneous. There's so much to be rightfully concerned about daily and so much we can do to uplift ourselves and others. But please, let's all remember to marry our purpose with copious amounts of joy and gratitude and light. Be your serious, but sparkly, self.

INVITATION

Light a sparkler. Celebrate what is to come. Watch that sparkler illuminate the dark. Then, remember that we are human sparklers lighting up the dark for one another. Aren't we lucky?

Celebrating the Journey

We begin the new year in the sign of Capricorn, the great sign of purpose and achievement. But just for today, let's not think about strategy, intention, or where we are headed. Let's not prepare, plan, or try to set ourselves up for success. Today, let's imagine that we are slowly but surely making our way up a mountain—a long journey over many days. Let's imagine there is no rush and there is plenty of time to soak in the beauty of the path. Let's appreciate how far we've already come and stop along the way to stretch and breathe. Today, let's remember simply that we are on our way. Let today be a day that celebrates our journey thus far—a bright and restful day to launch a beautiful year.

INVITATION

Today, take the time for loving reflection. Let's write using these three questions:

What feels more alive in you after this past year?

How does your heart feel walking into the New Year?

What's one quality you would love to grow in the year ahead?

Capricorn

Plans Can Feel Like Freedom

Structure and commitment can feel delicious. Sometimes a plan feels like freedom. Sometimes discipline and determination are the perfect antidote to lethargy or depression. Capricorn invites us to live on purpose and to be purposeful about how we spend our time and energy. Let's use Capricorn to feel our uprightness and authority, our leadership potential. If the going has been tough, let's use today to reconnect, commit to ourselves and our vision. Let's take a step. Let's choose to breathe in certainty and feel the gift of Capricorn, this grounded, earthy sign.

INVITATION

Today is a good planning day. How do you like to record upcoming plans and events? Do you love a beautiful calendar? Spend some time envisioning the days and months ahead. Put a few little plans in place. Remember, you can always change them if need be. Use this day to start to bring structure to your year.

Trusting the Present Pace

We wake to the cool, clear light of this earthy sign. Yes, there is something sobering and solo about Capricorn, but there's also a deep and authoritative resolve. We plan and proceed. We feel our inherent strength. We commit and work hard. We feel our own steady breath and move forward with clarity. We remind ourselves to trust the present pace. We are in for the entire journey. Let's not let obstacles throw us off course. Let's proceed. Let's try to see the biggest picture of this journey and trust ultimate fruition. Steady as she goes.

INVITATION

I invite you to stop in this moment, place both hands on your heart and quietly say, "I trust the pace of my life. I trust I am doing enough." Feel how you are standing tall. Feel your wise and loving self leading the way into your day.

Capricorn

Allowing for Softness

Capricorn can often be very hard on itself. Sometimes, it needs to remember its softness. The sign opposite Capricorn is Cancer and Cancer can help Capricorn do just that. Cancer offers loving, nourishing energy to the sometimes stoic Capricorn. When these two signs work together, it's a beautiful thing. Cancer reminds us that it's OK and in fact, deeply necessary to express what we feel. And Capricorn helps us by holding healthy boundaries and a safe, clear space to process.

INVITATION

Put this book down and wrap your arms around yourself. Take three deep breaths and direct great care and love inward. Let your shoulders drop and your face soften. Feel your hands as loving hands. Then take another breath, look out into the day, and move into your day with clarity and confidence from a place of fullness.

Our Capricorn Friends

Here are all the reasons it's great to have a Capricorn friend:

1. They are extraordinarily responsible and always do what they say they will do.

2. They value your time.

3. They are great at making plans and following through. They love to be in charge; and sometimes it's lovely to leave things in someone else's hands.

4. They will love you in all kinds of practical ways. Need to paint your kitchen cabinets? Your Capricorn pal will show up for the job.

5. They want to achieve and be great at what they do. They may inspire you to do the same.

6. They are generally very good with money. They know how to make it, and they're willing to share their know-how.

7. They are serious about loving you and take you seriously. They've got your back big-time.

8. They're strong, clear, and determined, and they work hard.

Yay for our Capricorn pals!

INVITATION

Reach out to your Capricorn pals to tell them you love them and why!

Saturn

The planet Saturn rules Capricorn, and carries the energy of the father. Sometimes that father voice is harsh and demanding. But the voice of the kind father is available to each of us. We can grow that voice within us. Today, let's allow the energy of the father to encourage us in its kindest, strongest Saturn way: "I see you. I see how hard you are working. I want you to be patient. You do not need to push. It's enough. I see your good work. You are doing your part. There is and will be fruition. I love you."

INVITATION

My friends, what clear, kind, potent message does Saturn have for you today? Write yourself a letter from your kind parent self—that place of clear, calm, direct knowing. Write encouraging words that give you structure and help you trust your own authority.

What Sets You Right

What sets you right? When you are feeling chaotic or out of balance, what grounds you? What makes your next step possible? What gets you back on track? Capricorn can help us pay attention to the choices we make that can lend a certain structure or clarity to our day—choices that help quiet the chaos. Capricorn helps us clarify what is important (and what is not) and allows us to move forward with more simplicity. It quiets us down enough that we can choose the next right step.

INVITATION

Today, gather some practical reset suggestions to help yourself align with your inner needs. Make a reset list in your phone notes or somewhere that's easy to access. Make sure to keep the list simple and direct. Use the list to remind yourself of the simple steps to course-correct when you most need them. Here are some examples to get you started: Make a cup of tea. Walk around the block. Read a poem out loud. Focus on your breath. Go outside and look at the sky or something beautiful in nature. Call a friend whom you know will hold you gently.

Inner Monologues

This is often the inner monologue of a Capricorn:

> *There's a lot to do and it's got to be done well.*
> *There's no use feeling sorry for myself. I'm always*
> *up for hard work. I have so much I want to accom-*
> *plish. I am patient and I will keep at it until I reach the*
> *heights I set for myself. I plan. I manage. I show up.*
> *Sometimes I think, If I don't, who will?*

If you relate to this, promise me something: I know you are a tender creature who takes things rather seriously, but do stop on occasion on your mountain climb and pick some wildflowers or take off your boots and backpack and sunbathe on a rock.

INVITATION

Sometimes when we consider a metaphorical mountain summit, we only think of the top or the end goal: achievement, success, power. Instead, challenge that inner monologue that aligns success with constant output. Think of the mountain in another way. Say to yourself, *I'm on the mountain of joy. I'm climbing the mountain of love. I'm on a journey up the mountain of learning to love myself, and that is enough.*

It's Time

It's time to stop rushing. Time unfolds as time unfolds, and rushing won't get us there any sooner (but it will ensure that we arrive exhausted and depleted). It's time to stop comparing ourselves or our work to anyone or anything. We each have our path. Every moment spent feeling less than or somehow not enough is wasted. It's time to loosen our grip and feel greater pleasure and peace on a daily basis. It's time to feel held by love; feel how the very earth supports us every moment, how it whispers support through birdsong and breeze and cloud-streaked skies.

INVITATION

Let's write: "It's time to . . ." Here are some suggestions to get you started: It's time to carve out room for solitude and listen to what wants to move through me. It's time for deeper and deeper layers of trust. It's time to accept that I don't have to have it all figured out and that vulnerability is integral to growth.

Capricorn

Boss Hat

Let's put on our boss hat. Let's recognize our inherent power, feel the strength and structure of our bones keeping us upright, and make some decisions. Let's be the progress we yearn for in our lives. We can say, "This. Now. It's happening." Or, "I'm on it. I'm picking up the phone. I'm asking the question. I'm making the date." Let's open the door to the next chapter of our lives and walk in like we mean it. We can walk strong, walk tall. We can say, "The time has come."

INVITATION

Make a decision today—just one small decision—and then act on it in some way, large or small. Capricorn wants practical action. We have to rely on ourselves to believe that what we want is possible and to take tangible steps to make it happen.

Sweet Potato Pie

How do we begin our day? Do we talk to ourselves in a loving way or do we just boot ourselves out of bed? What if we tried to think or say a few loving things to ourselves before we put on our adult faces and headed out to brave the day? We greet our loved ones with all kinds of sweet nicknames: "Hi, love," or "Good morning, sweet potato pie." What if we showed this love and tenderness to our own sweet selves?

INVITATION

This morning, instead of crinkling your brow and sighing an enormous *I've got so much work to do* sigh, try thinking: *Good morning, love. Have some fun today, sweet potato pie.* Have fun coming up with a few loving, playful names for yourself and sprinkle them into your self-talk today, buttercup.

Capricorn

You Are Not Alone

One of the greatest opportunities under Capricorn is the practice of surrender. There is a self-sufficiency in Capricorn's energy that can prevent us from fully accepting another's help. Capricorn's standard response when someone offers help is simply to refuse. "I've got this," is Capricorn's common refrain. The more we practice receiving or allowing for support, the more joyful life becomes. We surrender the mask of self-sufficiency and control. We open up to naming and expressing our feelings and vulnerabilities. In doing so, we become more free.

INVITATION

Today, practice being open to others—open to assistance, guidance, kindness, and grace. Practice saying yes to any offer of help today. Let someone open the door, carry something for you, or get you coffee. You have nothing to prove by doing it all alone.

Long-Term Optimist

My father called himself a short-term pessimist and a long-term optimist. In other words, things look quite bleak right now, but we'll figure them out. Capricorn is a great teacher of patience. It is connected to time and its passage. It teaches that there is no particular state that will last forever. It says, "Take it step by step, listen within, see it through, breathe through constriction." And also, "See the entire path and not just the stop on the way." Perspective is a great healer. Patience is a great ally.

INVITATION

Let's make Capricorn real today for all of us. Write for 15 minutes about one or both of these prompts and share your thoughts with a friend.

I commit to . . .

I am patient with . . .

Capricorn

Redwoods

The oldest redwood tree is about 2,500 years old. There are other tree species that are older, but redwoods have my heart. When I think about a redwood, I fall silent. There's something majestic and upright, watchful and wise about it. It seems to say, "I have witnessed everything. I have endured fire, war, loss, and resurrection. I stand witness to the passage of time." Redwoods have the strength to support many other redwoods. Their roots are interlocked, extend great distances, and support one another beneath the surface. So, though they seem to stand alone, their roots commingle and cooperate, and their treetops touch. They are deeply connected. Capricorn emanates that same patience and fortitude. It understands what it is to be tested, weather the storm, and silently prevail. It also learns that it has allies connected by the deepest roots and truest branches and it doesn't always have to stand solo.

INVITATION

Commune with a part of nature that symbolizes vastness and perspective to you, such as the ocean, the view from a mountaintop, or a forest of ancient trees. Remember the sky is always available and it has its own ever-changing magic. Allow the natural world to soothe every stressed place inside today.

Rules

Capricorn generally likes to follow the rules. Sometimes it's good to do an inner inventory about what rules we'd like to adhere to more and what rules have outlived their time. Here are some Capricorn questions to consider:

What are the rules you have chosen to live by?

Are they serving or confining you?

Are there rules you'd like to break or repeal?

What's your first liberating step?

INVITATION

Journal today and explore these four questions.

Our Own Authority

Capricorn invites us to consider our relationship with authority. Are we our own authority? Do we give our authority away? Do we cast someone else as the one in charge? Do we rebel? Do we speak up? Capricorn asks us what it would mean to be the authority in our own life story, to call the shots, to make the plan. If we tend to be commitment-shy about our work or relationships, it invites us to dip our toe in the commitment pool. It asks us to consciously, clearly, and powerfully choose our own next step.

INVITATION

When you think *in charge*, who comes to mind? Who do you defer to? Would you move through your day differently if you were the one in charge? What would it feel like to be the leader of your own life?

Peak Experiences

Capricorn gives us the capacity to do hard work that pays off. Capricorn helps us get it done. Have you ever felt connected to something greater than yourself? Have you felt exhilaration, relief, and pride for making it to the peak of the mountain, literally or figuratively? Have you felt joyous after the determined hike? Have you felt you can see your life more clearly from above? Don't put off what you know you are here to do. The time is here and now, and every step matters, no matter how small.

INVITATION

Sometime today, stand outside. Lift your arms to the sky. Rotate 360 degrees. Breathe. Carry the clarity and beauty of the summit within your heart. Let it whisper to you.

Capricorn

Gentle Now

Gentle now. No need to hurry. Let's be tender with our hearts, patient with our plans. So much is possible, but all in good time. All in good time. Let's start by listening, start by opening, start by asking. Let's exhale and make room for all that is to be, make room for all we are becoming. We are in the process of becoming someone new. Right now. Let's close our eyes and open them again slowly and see all things new. Let's see with soft eyes—eyes that receive and wonder and love. It's a new day. Walk gently into it.

INVITATION

All throughout today, invite softening. Invite a softer gaze. Invite softer shoulders, softer breath. Try to make everything easier, gentler, and less effortful.

Capricorn and Aquarius

Aquarius is always a breath of fresh air after the intensity and focus of Capricorn. As we move into Aquarius season, we feel a greater sense of freedom and perspective. We want to circulate. We feel lighter. Aquarius reminds us that we all have something of worth to share with one another and the best way to evolve is together. Aquarius is not a solo climber, but rather one who looks out for his fellow human every step of the way. We are preparing to enter the season of group work!

INVITATION

Tomorrow we start down the mountain into the valley where we share what we learned during Capricorn season. Now is the time to be on the lookout for true allies. Begin to think about the people with whom you would like to work or build something new together.

Capricorn

Aquarius

Welcoming Aquarius

Today, we welcome Aquarius, an air sign associated with mental brilliance, objectivity, originality, and group work. Aquarius at its best is a sign of great service in which we wish to play our part. Aquarius at its worst can also feel alone and aloof, rebellious, and steeped in its differences. The truth is, we are each one of a kind, but we are all also one united humanity. Ideally our uniqueness serves the whole with great generosity instead of rebelling for rebellion's sake. Aquarius longs for its true group of allies— soul-resonant friends who can journey through this life together.

INVITATION

Who are your true allies—past and present—who align with your soul song? Who are the people who want to create and play with you? This is the month to rally the troops and create magic together. Start with a coffee date with one pal and build from there!

Aquarius

The Great Circle

Hello, community. Hello, friends. Hello, fellow humans. Aquarius invites us to feel the ways we are connected beyond family, beyond blood. It asks us to remember that we are living at a time when we each must learn to love and cherish humanity as a whole. We can firmly disagree with ideas and actions of our fellow humans, but have to somehow learn to love the whole lot of us. We can work to make things better for us all. Aquarius does not have a chosen few. The best of Aquarius regards all with eyes of equality, and wishes ultimately for everyone to find their true place in the great circle.

INVITATION

A circle is profound and deeply healing. When we stand or sit or dance in a circle, we see everything. We are physically open to everyone. Next time you stand or sit in a circle, notice how it feels to be a part of it.

Something Good

Aquarius is the water bearer and wants to offer and circulate the waters of life. The "water" can be information, actual nourishment, or wisdom; Aquarius wants to share what it has for the benefit of all. It also always wants to improve current conditions. What is the "something good" you'd like to pour forth today?

INVITATION

What part can you play to make the day a little better for all you meet? Circulate some good today. Leave a letter of encouragement in a public place for a stranger. Write three snail-mail cards for no reason but to brighten someone's day. Send a little money to someone for a special treat. Bake cupcakes and bring them to work. Have fun with it!

Breaking Our Own Rules

We have all experienced times in our lives when we took an unexpected path, when we surprised ourselves or broke our own rules. Sometimes, those moments are big, like when I decided at the age of 29 to leave my job and become a full-time astrologer. But those moments can also be small, like canceling plans or saying yes to an unexpected invitation. Aquarius asks us to experiment in our lives every day and to surprise ourselves with a willingness to try to the new. Each reinvention opens the door to a new chapter.

INVITATION

Share or write about your unexpected paths or choices, and then try two little experiments or detours today! Take a different route to work, try a new coffee shop—break your rules for what you think today should look like.

Good Work

It's a great day to gather with purpose—to get down to work with any team, community, or artistic group. We are needing and wanting to gather in the name of something greater than our individual selves. There is a desire to relate, exchange, and collaborate. Aquarian energy doesn't want to isolate. It wants to say, "Who are you? And how are you?" And "Want to do some good work together?" It's a perfect day to dive in.

INVITATION

Today, if gathering is not possible, then sit down and brainstorm about the groups you'd like to engage, or create when the time is right. What collaboration is meant to be?

Aquarius

Joyfully Muddy

Have you ever run a team race with a small group of friends? It's so very aquarian. You're a band of brothers and sisters looking out for each other, laughing, getting dirty and exhausted. There are moments when you're scared to go on and others have to talk you through. There are moments when you get to lend a hand to another. It's messy and hard and hilarious and inspiring. This is Aquarius: this support, this camaraderie, this all-in-it-together, this common cause that keeps us curious and helps us grow.

INVITATION

Groups can buoy us. If there's something that you've been wanting to try, but haven't quite dared to try solo, see if you can gather a group (at least three people) to do it with you. Invite a team to support your dream.

I Can No Longer Be Contained

Here are a few lines of my poem, "I Can No Longer Be Contained."
This is a very Aquarian poem and I recommend reading it out loud.

I am a woman in my prime,
Like a number that cannot be divided.

It's time to own it,
Full out time to
Unfurl,
Uncurl,
Dance it out,
Dance it in,
love.

I can't stand still.
Don't want to.
It's not about composure
It's about composing.

I am am breathing now
And speaking now
And my throat has become a
Tunnel of love . . .

INVITATION

You can read the whole poem online at www.heidirose.com/poetry or
in my book *Wild Compassion.* Use the title of the poem as your writing
prompt for today. Start with, "I can no longer be contained" and go
from there.

Grant Yourself Permission

Today, shake a leg. Bust loose. Free yourself from constraint. Grant yourself permission. Fly the coop. Say yes. Say yes, again. Say no way. Say hello. Imagine yourself in another life entirely. Fully embrace the ride of your own life. Feel free. Celebrate your allies. Talk with your foes. Make a new friend. Bust a move. Sing together. Change an old pattern. Surprise yourself. Share something. You are gloriously unique.

INVITATION

Allow yourself a little more wiggle room today. Play in the realm of the unexpected. Choose one of the suggestions above and grant yourself permission to break a few of your own rules.

Thirsty

We are all thirsty: for love, wisdom, kindness, intelligence, truth-telling, and many for actual food and water. How can we provide for one another? How can we share resources with one another? Let us hold these questions in our hearts and stay open to inner answers.

INVITATION

Grab a journal. Ask yourself, "What do I pour forth? What is uniquely mine to offer to those who thirst, and how am I thirsty? Who or what might quench that thirst?" Start thinking about your friends and family. Use this format: "I could offer Kathy a ride to work. I could offer Susan a bouquet of flowers for her birthday. I could offer Kate help with her applications." Then try, "I could ask Elizabeth to help me make food for the party. I could ask David to edit my essay. I could ask Jim to help me raise money for the homeless."

Aquarius

Tiny Steps

So often we feel like we're not nearly bold or innovative or cutting-edge enough. Aquarius is so much about charting new territory that it's easy to feel that we are uninspiring or bland instead of electrically alive. But remember, repetition is good. We don't always have to be reinventing the wheel. Tiny steps in a good direction are still steps. A tiny step might be a deep cleansing breath, instead of a collapsed sigh. A tiny step might be a scrawled ten minute brainstorm on a page. A tiny step might be a phone call seeking support or encouragement. A tiny step might be one email sent to a significant person who could be helpful in your big vision. A tiny step is an internal kind word for your brave self in the world.

INVITATION

In the months where air signs rule, it's good to stop moving occasionally to catch our metaphorical breath. Then we can choose the next tiny step forward.

Our Aquarius Friends

Here are the reasons it's great to have an Aquarius friend:

1. They are undeniably themselves, one of a kind, totally original.

2. They color outside the lines and follow their own uncharted paths.

3. They often have a wild, free, unique way of moving through the world that inspires us all to be more true to ourselves.

4. They always have a more objective or unusual perspective that helps solve seemingly unsolvable problems.

5. They stand up for equality and the richness of diversity.

6. They love the cutting edge, what is new, fringy, or outside the status quo. This love of discovering the new helps us keep growing.

7. They can detach from overly emotional situations and offer wisdom or rational solutions.

8. They will rally and stand with community.

9. They love friendship.

Celebrate your Aquarius pals today!

INVITATION

Reach out to your Aquarius friends to tell them you love them and why!

The Wilderness of You

Today, explore the wilderness in you—the wild, the untamed. Explore the part that you've relegated to a back burner or swept under a rug. Have you been wanting to paint bold colors on huge canvases, but have never picked up a paintbrush? Go buy a canvas and a tube of paint. Have you wanted to rock climb, but never hoisted yourself off the ground? You know what to do. Be a bit bold today, a bit eccentric. Call yourself a little crazy. It's liberating. Reach out to someone you consider edgy. Reach out to your own edgy self. Think outside your daily box. Refuse to be contained. Refuse to contain yourself.

INVITATION

Make a toast to yourself at breakfast: Rules for the day? There are no rules! Throw an inner party for yourself. Make it a surprise party. Call a friend who you haven't talked to in years and say, "Catch me up." You get it: Shake it up. Wake yourself up. Don't try to accomplish anything. Go in search of a little awe and wonder. Do something that invites you to feel free.

Innovation

Sometimes limitation leads to innovation. Aquarius loves nothing more than carving out something new from old parts. It's like that scene in the film *Apollo 13* when there's something wrong with the space capsule and they have to fix it in space. So, down below on Earth, a group of scientists gather around a table and look at an odd assortment of things they know the astronauts have on board that they can use to fix the problem. They have to be brilliantly creative and open to using unexpected materials to save the day. And they succeed. What do we have that we can use to reinvent our lives? Is there possible joy, ingenuity, and innovation by proceeding in a new way? We can be both problem solvers and innovators. So much is possible.

INVITATION

Have a brainstorming session about a problem you've yet to solve. Don't edit yourself at all. Sprawl on the floor and think about the problem. Use a big purple marker to scribble ideas on a page. Sprint around the block and then think about the problem. Shake up your usual inner routine. Call someone who you don't usually turn to for help and ask them what they think. Innovate!

Gather

Why do we choose to gather? It's an opportunity to see one another deeply, to bear witness, to listen. It's a chance to safely unpack the contents of our hearts and have them held with care. It's an opportunity to show up new, different, to strengthen our emotional muscles, to say, "This is who I am in this moment. See me as I am. And I promise to do the same." Gathering promotes real growth and deep delight if the circle is held with fierce love. When we gather with the intention of helping one another, magic happens.

INVITATION

Plan a gathering, big or small. Who would you like to attend? Would you like to have a theme for the gathering? What would you like people to bring?

Quiet Now

It's OK. It's going to be OK. Everything that feels broken or raw or not enough, let it be. Rock it to sleep. Smoothe your brow. Everything is in the process of unfolding, evolving, mending. Nothing stays broken forever. Every ache, every sadness will find its way to healing, to softening. Find kind, gentle words for yourself this morning. We are all in bud. We are all finding our way to be touched by the sun. We're all slowly daring to open. We are all brave and scared, broken and whole, tired and renewed, hopeless and full of promise. Quiet now, loves. Start your day gently. Stay as soft and open as you are in sleep. Do not pick up your burdens yet. Walk lightly into this new day. It is already whispering its gifts. Put your hand on your heart and breathe.

INVITATION

Read the above slowly and out loud. Let the words fully resonate within you.

Aquarius

The State of Your Union

We've all heard of the State of the Union address, but have we ever thought about the state of ourselves? What if we stood before our loved ones and were as honest as possible about the state of ourselves. What would we choose to talk about first? Work, love? What are the first thoughts that come to mind about how we are at this moment in our life? Are we tender? Are we divided? Are we bereft? Is our economy thriving? Are we speaking up for ourselves in negotiations? Do we have allies? What can we be proud of that we've accomplished in the last months? Can we give ourselves a standing ovation for work well done? Where do we next need to put our loving attention? Is there someone in our life who needs our love and wisdom? What is the state of our union?

INVITATION

Let's write. The prompt is (you guessed it): "the state of my union."

For the Good

Aquarius is an air sign and it rules the distribution of information. It rules the internet, social media, and technology in general; it spreads the word quickly. Innovation and experimentation rule the day. Aquarius stands for freedom in all forms, freedom to express, freedom to be who we are without apology, freedom to change. The opportunity is, of course, to use that freedom and ability to connect quickly and powerfully, almost instantaneously, for the good. We could change the whole culture of social media one post, one message at a time.

INVITATION

What good work or good words might you distribute today? Alexandra Franzen, writer, speaker, and entrepreneur, has a newsletter that is always filled with good news and uplifting messages. Every link in it leads to a little delight. When I open one of her newsletters, I know I will receive beauty, bounty, laughter, and helpful information. Check her out. And let's all try to offer inspiring connections to others when we have the chance.

Share

The energy of Aquarius has a lot to do with sharing resources and distribution. At the beginning of the day, let's ask ourselves what we can share. Maybe it's something tangible, like a cookie or a sandwich. Maybe it's information or advice that can be of value to another. Maybe we could share a ride or share laughter. Sharing opens the door to friendship and dynamic collaboration.

INVITATION

What can we share with someone else today that makes our world a little more intimate or kind? A piece of music or a poem, a smile, a hug, a park bench? Our thoughts, our love, our home? Pick something and do it today.

Brothers and Sisters

Aquarius is the sign of brotherhood and sisterhood. Brothers and sisters often share the longest relationship in a lifetime. Aquarius says, "Only when we begin to look upon each other another as brothers and sisters of the human family, will we truly heal and evolve." Yes, brothers and sisters find one another infuriating at times, but they also are likely to work on the relationship because they are family. We can all practice recognizing that despite our differences, we are part of one great struggling, broken, loving, chaotic, suffering, growing family.

INVITATION

Today, let's do a day-long exercise. Throughout the day, practice looking at someone new and think, *You are my brother*. Today, breathe in and think *You are my sister* as someone passes you on the sidewalk. Sometimes we can work to build greater unity and compassion by beginning internally. When we change how we see the world, we act differently within it.

Uranus and Jupiter

Uranus is one of the rulers of Aquarius. Uranus loves to shatter outdated forms. It instigates change. Aquarius at its best says, "Don't get stuck in any old rut, bust it open and try something new." Then if it works, we can offer the new in the name of progress. Jupiter is another ruler of Aquarius, and Jupiter is known for its generosity, amplifying the Aquarian desire to share. It promotes cooperation, combined effort, and progress. These two planets allow us to reach beyond our own little selves and help others live well and evolve. Aquarius says, "The days of me and mine must be over. The era of we and our must begin—our planet, our human family, our opportunity to thrive."

INVITATION

Read the poem "'Sometimes a Wild God" by Tom Hirons. Read it out loud. It's long but potent. Imagine inviting the wild god Uranus to your table to shake things up.

First Impressions

When we sit in a circle, there is often someone we are drawn
to, another that we are curious about. There may be someone
with whom we do not feel a resonance. There's another person
we know that could help us grow and maybe someone that just
immediately rubs us the wrong way. The beauty of a circle of
humans is that all these feelings, attractions, and curiosities exist
at once. Today, let's consider doing some investigative or healing
work around that friction or attraction in our communities, our
friendship circles, our work. In the true spirit of Aquarius, let's
practice setting aside our preferences or instinctual likes and dis-
likes to empower the group and grow its love and consciousness.

INVITATION

Practice both surrendering *and* acting on first impressions. Next
time you are in a circle or a meeting or a gathering, notice your inner
process. With whom do you immediately want to connect? Notice
judgment, hesitation, or fear. Work to challenge those first impressions and see what is underneath. Have a conversation with someone you are sure you will not like. See what happens.

Aquarius

It's Going to Be a Good Day

Have you ever tried waking and, sitting up in bed, taking a breath, and quietly saying, "It's going to be a good day"? I've been practicing this lately, because otherwise I find myself sighing and hurling myself out of bed like I'm about to face an onslaught of duty and nonstop doing. Sometimes, I actually believe myself when I sit up and invite in a different kind of day. Aquarius allows the new. It vitalizes and vivifies. It reminds us that we can remodel, renew, renovate, or reinvent our lives whenever we choose. Add the electric to your ordinary day. Share your spunk. Fly your freak flag. Do it for love. Be alive, awake, and invite in the fresh day that is knocking.

INVITATION

Let's write. Start with these simple words: "It's going to be a good day." Work with the idea of creating and cooperating with your day. You can choose how you wish to move within the unfolding hours.

True Blue

Aquarius rules friendship. Take a minute right now and think of a friend who knows you, loves you, and has walked through a dark hour with you. Feel the lines of light and gratitude and love that connect you. Feel how we have each been lifted and sometimes carried by beloved friends. Notice how being truly seen and witnessed by dear friends is one of the greatest gifts. To be a friend is to love freely, to grow another person through our love. Today, let's celebrate the friends who have loved us, grown us, supported us, and held us all along the way. We are blessed to have had even one true blue friend.

INVITATION

Let's do a friendship review on the page. Start in your childhood and remember a friend. Honor that friend by naming a quality that they gifted you with. Remember how they strengthened you or lightened you up. Then, as if documenting a journey, think of another friend and name how they brought their goodness to you. Even if, in your remembering, you happen upon a friendship that ended or that brought you pain, think about how you changed or evolved as a result of that friendship.

Aquarius

Set Down Your Honorable Load

In my poem "Wild Compassion," I end with these words:

Give it away,
The stranger,
Your day,
All of it.

Die into the darkness
That will swallow your pain
With its fierce love.

Set down your honorable load.

Then trust this,
Morning Light
Will touch your cheek.

You need only turn
Ever so slightly toward it.

INVITATION

Give yourself a fresh start today. Turn toward the light that wants to touch your cheek. What does that mean for you? How might you give yourself a second chance? If you'd like, you can read the whole poem (try it out loud!) at www.heidirose.com/poetry.

Detached

What do you think of when you hear the word *detached*? Do you think aloof and removed, or simply not attached to outcomes? All can be true of Aquarius. It's true that Aquarius often works from a distance. It sees the whole picture. It absents itself from the details of the problem so it can solve it. It tends to observe rather than immerse. Aquarius can pull back and look at and love humanity as a whole, without a lot of complex personal drama. Aquarians consider the welfare of the whole.

INVITATION

Just for a moment, let's experiment. Feel yourself in the thick of your life with all its cares and worries. Focus on yourself or your little family. Now take a deep breath and pull back, zoom out, to look at your life and your community from a distance. What do you see? How does it feel? What does it bring up? Is there relief? What do you understand by detaching?

Aquarius

Beloved

Good morning and hello, love. Yes, you. Happy day of love among many days of love. Today, let's choose not to feel bereft of love in any way. Let's embody love, stand in love, stand as love. Let's not wait for it, but be it. Let's not stand outside it, but enter it. Let's fall in love twenty times today with a flower, a tree, a stranger, kind eyes, or a delicious breakfast. Yes, let's fall into love rather than standing at the edge and dipping our toes in. Let's crack open and shed some tears if we need to, rendering us more available to love. Tears are great softening agents and when our edges are soft, we feel a greater connection and warmth with all our fellow travelers. May this morning note be a big fat valentine to each and every one of you. I send you big love.

INVITATION

Take inspiration from www.moreloveletters.com and make ten anonymous valentines for strangers. Leave them at coffee shops or around your neighborhood or on public transit. Make someone's day with your little gesture of love.

Introduce Yourself

Let's embrace the spirit of Aquarius and create a name for ourselves that captures our essence. We can do it like this: "He who carries the wildness of horses." "They who are softening and surrendering." "She whose song dispels sorrow." "She who fiercely stands for justice." "They who shake us into action." "She who is feeling her way forward." Names can be superpowers. Aquarius wants to be a part of the group journey. What is your soul name today? Today, I am "she who surrenders what she *knows*, to uncover what she *feels*."

INVITATION

Share your name with a friend and invite others to create their own. Talk about what underlies the name. Talk about why the name is perfect for you at this moment in your life.

Friendship

Aquarius rules friendship. It reminds us how we lift one another, inspire and motivate one another to keep growing. How have your best friends showed up for you this year? What quality or qualities do some of your closest pals embody that inspire you? If we feel lonely in this moment, let us lovingly, exquisitely befriend ourselves.

INVITATION

What does it mean to offer friendship? What could we say about being a friend? Let's brainstorm together about how we can be a better friend to others and to ourselves. Here are some thoughts: Share gratitude, offer encouraging words, name the beauty that you see, even if you've just met. Tell the truth, find common ground, learn another language, look for hidden treasures. Be curious. What else?

A New World

These days, I want to write a new world. I want pen and ink to press love, truth, and civility into the book of our lives. I want us to remember that we are writing our history, our stories for generations to come. I want words spoken to call forth our humanity and not further forge divisions of hate. I want these daily ongoing earthquakes to wake us up to our own fragile and powerful selves. I want us to hold ourselves accountable for tiny transgressions and huge unfathomable ones and to remember that our every choice either contributes to chaos and division or invokes greater consciousness and care. Let us take a collective breath. Let's be wise. Let's be kind.

INVITATION

Let's write. Your prompt is: "I am fragile and powerful." Go for 15 minutes. Don't stop. Don't edit!

Pisces

Welcoming Pisces

Pisces is the great sign of unconditional love. It is an ocean of sensitivity, imagination, flow, and feeling. It is balm and redemption at its best, and escape, illusion, and isolation when it gets stuck. Pisces wraps up our *astrological* year. It is the winter that prepares us for spring. Pisces loves solitude and it flourishes when it has the space and silence necessary to connect with the divine. Pisces loves music and can follow the beauty of song to the highest, most loving realms. Pisces invites us to listen deeply to the music of our soul and share that music in every loving gesture. When in Pisces, we call upon our imagination and open ourselves to all inspiration that wants to flow through. We do our best to become a true conduit of compassion and love.

INVITATION

Pisces rules poetry and music. Every day this month, read a poem out loud or sing a song. Let's share our sensitivity through the voice. Let's move from silence to sound together.

I Set You Free

As the last sign of the zodiac, Pisces always brings a kind of letting go. It brings the melancholy of endings, the heartache of goodbye, the quiet of culmination. After the flurry of connection and community in Aquarius, we take a breather. We might spend time alone to replenish or reflect. We carry a sense of oneness in our heart and mind under Pisces, but it is simply felt and known. Pisces rules quiet meditation and contemplation. Words shared are less important than a deep feeling-sensitivity. We can look out to the ocean or gaze at the horizon or breathe in a mountain range and feel our small but significant place in the immensity of it all. We are one tiny light in a great vastness, but still we feel our part. We surrender to and are carried by the universal heartbeat— the great in-breath and out-breath of all that is.

INVITATION

This month think about what you're ready to let go of. You might need to leave a job or finally release a relationship in your life that you've needed to end for some time. Use the phrase "I set you free" and write for 10 minutes. What are you ready to set free?

Silence

What is your relationship to silence? Is there too much in your life? Not enough? Does it make you uncomfortable or do you crave it? Does it allow you to let down and soften or does it confront? I invite you to carve out some silence today. Close the door or go on a walk or find a big tree in a park and sit under it. Turn off your phone, close your computer, take a deep breath, and then just be with yourself. Try to be gentle. Try to be kind with yourself. Feel what the noise of your life has made it difficult to feel. You don't need any answers.

INVITATION

Listen to the whispers of your tender self in this intimate silence. What do you need? What do you love? What can you release into this silence? What can this silence offer you?

Pisces

Heaps of Self-Forgiveness

Pisces is: whispered devotion, spacious silence, heaps of self-forgiveness. Poetic confessions and tiny, sacred gestures. A pause from the push. Softening the armor. Melting the defense. Humility. Good work done in love. A meal made with devotion, food as loving nourishment. A song written for each of us. Lyrics we love. A song written on our hearts. The relief of truth, tender touch. Inhale, exhale, inhale, exhale. A sigh. An ocean walk at the water's edge. Whispers of ancestors, thankful tears, old love letters, new love letters. Cherishing. The beauty of the unknown. Infinite, unceasing love. A waterfall of grace.

INVITATION

Think about self-forgiveness. Write three things down on a page for which you are willing to forgive yourself. Breathe deeply as you write each word.

The Call of the Ocean

Let's all take a deep breath together right now. And another. Now let's imagine we are holding a conch shell to our ear and we begin to hear the call of the ocean. Imagine that the call awakens the ocean inside us, and we can feel our breath, like the waves, flowing in and out. Let's put ourselves at the ocean's edge and let the water wash over our feet. Is the ocean warm or cold? Does it soothe us or wake us up? Let's open our arms wide and receive the blessing of the water. Let's breathe in the perspective only the ocean can offer and see the light of the sun dance on the water as a gift for us. Let's notice how the sea meets the sky at the far horizon and feel that meeting as a kiss, a union within us. Let's feel how we are sea and sky. Breathe and surrender. Let's feel how vast we are.

INVITATION

Let's write: "The first time I saw the ocean . . ."

Pisces

Encourage

It's easy to feel discouraged in Pisces. I've noticed thoughts creep in like, "What's the use? It will never come together. This is exhausting. It's time to give up." If this flavor of Pisces seeps in, let's practice observing those feelings. Is it possible to experience ourselves as *having* those feelings but not *being* those feelings? I sometimes feel swallowed whole by feelings and struggle to get perspective. Pisces does rule the ocean, after all. It's easy to feel immersed. But today let's practice observing from the eye of the soul, which is centered on love. How can we be tender and uplift ourselves? I love the word *encourage* as it invites us to kindle the flames of the heart. When we gently encourage ourselves, we remember the spark of light that forever burns and warms us at the center of our being.

INVITATION

What truly uplifts you? Music, poetry, photography, the elegance of math? What songs or art pieces awaken something within that reminds you who you truly are? Inspiration often leads to a positive reengagement with the world. Today, seek out a little inspiration to uplift any flagging spirits.

Our Pisces Friends

Here are the reasons it's great to have a Pisces friend:

1. They deeply feel and understand you. They know when you need encouragement and compassion.

2. They're willing to listen and then listen more.

3. They care about the state of humanity. They feel the pain and need and offer their love.

4. They stand for and offer love.

5. They love their solitude and teach us all about the necessity of solo time.

6. They are sometimes poets or musicians or photographers offering their vast imagination through artistry.

7. They are dreamers and offer hope through their dreaming.

8. They teach us all about breathing into vastness and spaciousness and feeling connected to something greater than ourselves.

9. They will love you and love you and love you some more.

Big love to our Pisces friends.

INVITATION

Reach out to your Pisces pals to tell them how much you love them and why!

Mr. Rogers

We wake to feeling, flow, sensitivity, and silence. This is not a morning to leap into anything. Start slowly. Drink a cup of tea and listen to the wind or the birds or your breath or your heartbeat. Don't go back to sleep, but carry a quiet wakefulness throughout your day. Spend time today looking at someone or something through the lens of compassion. Seek to understand. Think about the iconic childhood educator Mr. Rogers. He was a double Pisces, repeatedly and lovingly asking us all, "Won't you be my neighbor?" And he meant it. He asked us all to be gentler and more welcoming with one another. He encouraged us to have a healthy, open, and positively directed relationship with our feeling life. So, invoke Fred Rogers today, his real compassion and care. If you feel low, put your hand on your heart and breathe in the love you already are.

INVITATION

Watch Fred Rogers' passionate plea when he testified before the Senate Subcommittee on Communications about public TV. See compassion in action.

Nameless

In my poem "Nameless," I explore who we are beneath all the things we name ourselves:

We are not who we say we are.
There are no words for that name, none full enough.
Our name is a symphony, a sunrise.
It is a name that holds all the sounds of silence.

We are not who we say we are
Though we insist it is so.

Maybe we should listen for the name
The sky has to offer, or the redwood.
It would be loving and infinitely simple.

Let's lay each name we've spoken
Into a great flame.

Let's soften the grasp on what is only ours
And breathe the terror, the flush of freedom.
Let's be nameless for a time
And listen.

INVITATION

Read this poem slowly and out loud. Savor each line.

Don't Be Afraid

It's said that the wonderful poet Seamus Heaney's last words to his wife were: "Don't be afraid." Let's not be afraid to express our full selves in this world or to speak what needs to be spoken. Let's not be afraid to press ourselves into the new world, shedding old behavior that no longer promotes growth. Let's not be afraid to take a full deep breath and leap, carve the words on the page, speak the truth. Let's not be afraid to surrender ourselves into the next unknown chapter. This is how we grow our light: by crossing the next threshold, and then the next. Let's not be afraid to live, to die into new life or be the heroine or hero of our own life journey. Don't shrink from its call. Don't be afraid, my friend.

INVITATION

Write "Don't be afraid" on a piece of paper. You can make it into a beautiful note for yourself or let it just be a Post-it note. Put it somewhere where you will see it daily. See how those words work on you.

The Realm of Grace

Whenever I write, think, or say "Pisces," I slow down almost immediately. I take a breath. I think, *Oh yes, I remember this quiet, silent place, this tender heart.* I begin to feel what is under the surface, the hurry of the day, or the press of the moment. Pisces's song is sacred, ancient, beckoning, and wise. As the last sign of the Zodiac, Pisces knows how to travel through difficulty and pain. It knows heartbreak. It knows loss. It also understands wholeness and asks us to surrender our fragmented selves to breathe together through the pain. It asks us to return to the well that is life-giving, the waters of kindness and compassion. Pisces is here to remind us that no one is outside the realm of grace. One breath, one felt exhale can return us to the warmth of our beating heart and the collective heart of humanity. So, when we are in Pisces, let's feel below the surface. Let's extend our sensitivity outward. Let's shed the tears that need to be shed for ourselves and all in pain. Then, let's take a deep life-giving breath and exhale nourishment for ourselves and for all who need grace on a wing.

INVITATION

Sit for a few minutes. Close your eyes and imagine breathing together with people across the globe. Remind yourself that you are not breathing alone, and that each breath is a shared breath. If this is a leap year, on February 29th, I invite you to flip through the book and stop when you wish! Let that message speak to you for the day. Or, write about all the ways you've made big leaps in your life!

Let the World In

Pisces invites us all to make boundaries less distinct. When we write under Pisces, we can fall into the page. When we walk and look up at an old beloved tree, we find ourselves one with the highest branches, touching the sky. Or we stand at the ocean's edge and feel our body to be water itself. We can even practice softening our face, our throat, our chest, our belly, and breathe to let the world touch us. We are all already so very good at being distinct, being singular, feeling our "I-ness". But Pisces invites us to feel far beyond ourselves and to feel our oneness with all that is. Pisces reminds us to let the world in, to let ourselves be touched by all its pain and beauty.

INVITATION

At any moment today, stop to regard something beautiful. And then allow yourself to stay with that beauty long enough that you begin to be a part of it. Breathe to let the beauty enter. Breathe to soften the edges. You can practice with a tree, a flower, or even a child. Practice oneness with the world around you.

Rain and Tears

Pisces rules water, including rain and tears. Rain and tears soften and grow us. They are both a blessing, a release, a kind of necessary letting go. After a good cry, we can feel our parched earth starting to blossom in a new and tender way. And when it rains, the land soaks it in. The colors of the flowers are brilliant after rain. It's like the earth is sighing in relief and beauty. As a result, Pisces time is receiving, melting, thawing time. Pisces asks us to open more deeply and completely to reveal all the soft and tender places that have been hidden and protected too long. So, on this Pisces day, let's open the earth of ourselves to the rain and blessings that want to fall. Who knows what will begin to grow and unfold?

INVITATION

Sometimes, just standing in the shower can be like standing in a rain of grace. It reminds you to let the tears fall and the feelings flow—to let the water wash away all you need not carry. You can also simply imagine yourself standing under a waterfall or in a great rainstorm and notice how your body begins to let go.

Pisces

Nestle

Start slow. Have your favorite morning beverage. Read the paper. Take an early morning walk. Stay in bed. Do what feels delicious. Snuggle. Curl in. Enjoy time out of time. Stretch. Yawn. Stay in cozy clothes as long as possible. Exhale. Amble. Don't rush. Don't even think too much. Breathe your day. Let the day lap at your toes like a warm, welcoming ocean. Let yourself soften. Nestle into the couch or stand in a spot of sunlight and turn your face toward the sun. Notice all that is good in your life today. Open your arms and embrace it.

INVITATION

Even if you are late for work or have a day filled with tasks, consciously and inwardly slow down. Bring comfort and quiet along for the ride of your day.

Little Boat

Let's imagine this. We are in a little boat in a vast body of water. We feel totally safe and supported. We are on our back, looking up at the sky. The sun is warm. We want to soak it in. Time is irrelevant. It is somehow silent but also filled with a thousand little sounds: the water against the boat, the cry of a bird, our own heartbeat. We know we can let go even further. We do. We see only the sky and we feel ourselves carried and buoyed by water, water, water. We find ourselves surrendering all we have been carrying. We find ourselves breathing more deeply. We feel ourselves exquisitely alone, and also completely held by all who love us. We trust this moment. There's nothing to do but give ourselves entirely to this moment. The sun is shining upon us, and an ocean of love is at our back. We are held and loved between sea and sky. We can let go. We can soften. We can let go. We can soften.

INVITATION

Let's write: "I'm letting go . . ." See where it takes you. Write for 15 minutes.

Pisces

The Feet

Pisces rules the feet. As we read this, let's pay meticulous attention to our feet on the ground. Let's feel our heel, our big toe. Let's feel perhaps where the arch lifts and doesn't touch. Let's feel the earth through our feet, the solidity, stability, and heft of the earth that is always holding us. Now let's keep feeling our feet, but say a quiet hello to our heart. Feel the sun of the heart and the love of the earth and breathe. Let's feel the ocean of our body, the vast feeling waters, but let the waters be still. We can allow the sun of our heart to shine on the still waters and feel ourselves rooted to the loving ground beneath us.

INVITATION

Take a walk today and let it be a blessing walk. Let gratitude or blessing be left in your wake. Touch the earth with your Pisces feet with a sense of wonder that we get to walk on this earth at all. Slow down enough to let your walk be one filled with gratitude and presence.

Are You in Love?

My beloved friend and extraordinary teacher Sofia Diaz will often ask, "Are you in love?" And just as everyone begins to answer a yes or no based on their relationship status, she asks, "If not, why not? Why are you not in love, this minute?" She means, of course, to broaden our definition of being in love, far beyond romantic love. I've come to love this question. Even at my most stuck, angry, and hopeless, I'm willing to ask, *How might I be in love in this moment?* Love abounds and is always knocking and wanting to soften our most resistant places. It whispers to us, cajoles, says, "Open your eyes." At any moment, we can fall in love with a person, a flower, a book, ourselves. Any moment, a new breath can usher in a waterfall of grace. Let's use the energy of Pisces to remember we are not bereft or alone or outside of love's embrace. We can stand in love because love is what we are.

INVITATION

Put your full, loving attention on something or someone today. Focus on simply giving or receiving love. Choose to be in love with something, anything, now, in this moment.

Rest

A Pisces day flows. It unfolds. It laps at our toes. It whispers and soothes and sings. A Pisces day allows time for naps, ambles, reading, and indoor or outdoor picnics. We might take a drive with no destination, plant some flowers, read poetry out loud to someone we love (including ourselves). We can sit in a cozy place with a cup of something delicious and just daydream, brew, stare into space, breathe, rest. A Pisces day begs for a good rest. It asks us to slow down and listen for what feels like a delicious next unfolding to our day.

INVITATION

What feels like rest to you? What feels restorative? Do that. Even if you have only 10 minutes in your day for some tangible rest, use that. Close your office door and take a nap. Step outside and away from your computer and move your body. Make yourself a healthy lunch. Restore yourself. Replenish, refresh, refill, renew, revive.

Pisces Questions

What part of you feels hidden?

Tell me about a tiny gesture of love you recently offered or received.

Tell me about a body of water that you love.

When did you last cry?

Name what you are willing to release.

What is no longer yours to carry?

What do you need to whisper to yourself right this minute?

INVITATION

Answer one or all of these questions today. Be sure to share at least one answer with a friend.

Pisces

Deep Below

Did you know that only 5 percent of our oceans have been explored? Did you also know that we spend millions more to explore outer space than our oceans? Now don't get me wrong. I'm all in favor of outer space exploration, but isn't it ironic that we've never explored 95 percent of the deep, dark, feminine, life-giving waters? Pisces of course, rules the ocean. It rules what is hidden below the surface. Pisces invites us into our own deep waters. It asks us to feel our fluidity and our permeability. It reminds us that we are each a mystery to be discovered. It whispers that with love we begin to unlock, unravel, uncover the mystery of ourselves and one another.

INVITATION

Let's write: "Below the surface . . ."

Pluto

If Pisces rules both love and endings, what might we each need to let go or end so that a greater love can present itself? What might we need to wrap up or complete? What pattern has outlived its purpose? What cycle must come to an end? Pluto is the esoteric ruler of Pisces and asks these very questions. Pluto is the great healer. It asks us to surrender and shed the tears that cleanse and release what is heavy within us. Let us use this Pisces day to begin to release what we've carried too long. Let's start a new cycle— emptied, open, lighter, and curious. Are we willing?

INVITATION

One way to shed or end a cycle is with fire. Fire is purificatory. We light a candle to end the darkness. We metaphorically burn that which locks us into a past that does not serve us. On this day in Pisces, do your best to burn your list of old grudges, even if they're with yourself. You might even write a few down and burn them in a candle flame. Start a new chapter, a little lighter, a little freer.

Let Love In

Pisces is the great sign of unconditional love. Sometimes, we feel gorgeously steeped in that love and other times we might feel bereft, alone, or isolated from the waters of love and compassion. During those times, how can we remember that the love is always a breath away? In Pisces, we have the exquisite opportunity to soften and receive and look at the world with gentler eyes. We all feel stuck and tired at points, but Pisces at its best whispers in our ear: *Let love in.* What if we looked at the world, instead of a person, as our beloved? Feel loved by the beauty of a flower. Feel loved by a stranger's kind smile. Offer love by listening. Offer love by opening a door. Whether we are in love or not, we can be *in* love every day.

INVITATION

Write a love letter—not to a person or a pet, but instead write to the sea, the sun, the sky, the tulips on your desk, or the tree in your backyard.

A Practice for Pisces

Here are a few steps to welcome the gifts of Pisces into our lives:

Feel and know the heart of another.

See their pain.

Speak potent, encouraging words without trying to fix anything.

Ever and always listen and offer understanding.

INVITATION

This is a tangible practice. Each of these steps is doable and practical. Try working with these steps today if given the opportunity. You may find that you spend time on just one of the steps, and that can be equally impactful.

On That Road

Here's a little dream for a Pisces day. We climb in our cars with our favorite music, ready to go. In this dream, we can each decide if we want a friend, a lover, or our solo selves along for the ride. We take off with no apparent destination and we sing the whole way. Outside, we pass wildflowers, mountains, oceans, fields of gold. We find that we are breathing deeply and are soothed by each breath. Nothing weighs too heavily today. Today, we drive and sing and dream and wonder. We let the horizon line beckon—an invitation to keep moving with a sense of possibility and curiosity. We allow moments of sadness to move in and through without too much attachment. We let joy in. We are easy. We welcome the unknown. We are kind to our traveling selves. Even if we have to be in an office all day today, let's close our eyes and, just for a moment, be on that road.

INVITATION

Even if you can't be on the road trip, listen to "road trip music" today. What makes you feel free and easy and expansive?

Time Is Not Linear

Recently, I sorted through a big box of old family photos. It left me feeling once again how time is not linear. My little girl self is alive in me now and my great grandmother's dreams whisper in my ear. We are forever healing our lineage forward and backward. We are forever on a path to forgive and be forgiven—to soothe the brow of our grandfather long passed or to encourage the fiery spirit of a child now present in our lives. Pisces yearns for wholeness and works to bring what is broken into understanding. Pisces seeks to end any cycle that does not lead to greater love.

INVITATION

Today, let some smallness within you begin to fade. Let it die. Let it dissolve. What might you soften or surrender today? Welcome something greater—something more true.

Shedding

We are quieter under Pisces, and it's easier to sense the sea of emotion inside us. I notice when I stop rushing and pushing and finally listen, the first wave of feeling is sadness. Tears are only shed when we feel present in the moment, but the waters are always flowing in Pisces. And after sadness comes a wave of self-compassion that allows a deeper rest and a deeper letting go. And this makes way for love. Pisces invites us to shed our many layers of protection until we stand as we are. And from that place, the only thing that makes sense is to give and receive the love we are. Our sadness cracks us open. That tenderness, then, offers a choice. Do we protect ourselves in our vulnerability or do we offer our understanding and love to one another?

INVITATION

Read the poem "Instructions for the Journey" by Pat Schneider. Read it slowly and out loud.

Pisces Love Letter

This is a Pisces love letter to a reeling world. We do not know how all will unfold. All we know in this moment is that we are capable of doing hard things. We are capable of treating one another with kindness. We know that we all feel afraid, that we all want to protect those we love. We know that sometimes life and all its pain feels huge, but our love can be equally so. I think too, we each know we have something to give—big or small. We each have something precious that can improve the day for another. Something is always breaking, but gold can seep through the cracks. We live in defining times. Let's offer the best of ourselves to ourselves and one another.

INVITATION

Rumi wrote, "Wherever you are, be the soul of that place." The words are an invitation to arrive where you are, shed the inessential, and listen. They ask you to show up and turn your attention outside yourself. What shares the space with you? When you stand as a soul of a place, you can bless that place as your feet touch the earth. Notice what you bring to whatever place you stand today.

I'll Meet You There

Let us stand at the ocean's edge together. How is the water today? Is it endlessly calm and tranquil? Are the waves crashing to shore? Do you want to wade in to test the temperature? Do you want to run in and shock the system? Do you plunge or do you slowly glide? Are you alone? Are you with friends? Is it terrifying or quieting? How does the ocean feel to you as you breathe it in? Now let the ocean be love—a vast sea of Pisces unconditional love. It is ever and always lapping at your shores, beckoning you to surrender to its vastness. Sometimes it's enough to sit in the sand and let it wash over your feet. And some days it's so warm, you just have to submerge yourself to float and breathe and stare at the sky.

INVITATION

Let's write: "I'll meet you at the ocean's edge." See where it takes you.

A Pisces Day

Here are some things to do on a Pisces day.

1. Find a poem you love and read it out loud.
2. Listen to your favorite music—maybe an entire album.
3. Take a long shower or bath.
4. Go to the beach.
5. Write a love letter of any kind to yourself, your mother, your friend, your lover.
6. Take a picture of something you find beautiful and send it to a friend.
7. Spend some time in silence.
8. Whisper some nice things to yourself.
9. Stretch.
10. Spend some time with a soft furry creature.
11. Have a cup of tea.
12. Extend loving care to someone who could use your help.
13. Shed any tears that need shedding.
14. Be tender with yourself and others today.
15. Inhale love, exhale love.

INVITATION

Choose at least one of the above suggestions and practice it today. Let Pisces work on you!

The Chord

Pisces prepares us for Aries. It says, "Soon enough you will be diving in and rushing forward and taking action. Let's be sure we notice this moment in all its subtleties before plunging into the next one. Let's soften into this particular moment in time and love everything and everyone we can." Once, my sweet niece, a Pisces, sat by the ocean with her guitar. The sun was setting and she told me she wanted to listen for the chord, the note, the tone the ocean was singing at that moment. It was cold and beautiful and perfect. I sat and listened with her until it got dark. When in Pisces, listen for the chord or the message the earth is always singing to us. Tune in to the Pisces vastness before setting forth. Be one with the ocean or the sky so you can carry it within on your Aries quest.

INVITATION

Let's write: Use this prompt: "Before I say goodbye. . . "

Acknowledgments

Big love and boundless gratitude to Casey Wilson, friend and champion, for setting up the first conversation that made this book possible; Cristina Garces, my editor, for saying yes and offering kindness and guidance along the way; my agent, Taylor Haggerty of Root Literary, who made it all easy.

The whole extraordinary book team—Daniel Barreto, Rachel Harrell, Tera Killip, Jessica Ling, and Gabriel Martinez—your artistry, editorial eye, and excellent support brought this book to life!

Wyoh Lee for helping me grow my business with such brilliance for seven years; Erin Schlabach for bold envisioning and attention to all the details; Lindsey Smith for believing in and publishing *Zodiac Love Letters*; Meredyth Hunt, retreat magic maker; Ellen Fondiler, planter of seeds; Renee Colvert, endless encouragement; Bruce Gelfand, writing teacher and dear friend.

Valeri Pfahning, Lynn Jordan, Kendra Smith, Dene Mason, Adriana Rizzolo, Anne Parker, Caitlin Muelder, Kristine Oller, Rachel Putter, Patricia Lakatos, Patrice Egleston, Michelle Shaw, Gisela Burquet, Kellynn Meeks, Holly Burrell, Paula Cole, Susan Madruga, Natalie Kalustian, Juliana Bellinger, Kathy Blandin, Jules Blaine Davis, Joanna White, Edie Cortese, Bruna Maia, Sharon Little, Kathy Duggan, Stacey Jacobs. You are my sisters and forever friends and I love you hugely.

To all the Radiant Life Retreat participants who attended retreats over the past twelve years: I am so deeply grateful for you. And to a generous, loving Instagram community that nourished the seeds of this book for over five years.

June Diane Raphael, Jessica St. Clair, Lennon Parham, Kulap Vilaysack, Matt McConkey, Vera Santamaria, Morgan Walsh, Elizabeth Laime, Kate Spencer, Olivia Hansen—you are huge and ongoing blessings in my life.

Elizabeth Rainer and Jolie Kobrinsky—my lifelines for thirty years.

Aja, Jade, Sage, Ben, Elizabeth, Jim, Nancy, Virginia, Richard, Susannah, Ben, Brennon, Mat, Katy, Tuija, Siri, Tara—I am blessed that you are my family.

Uncle Leon, you made so much possible.

Mom and Dad, I am the luckiest of daughters. I love you.

Andrew, Dylan, and Kate, my forever loves.

For Sofia Ophelia Diaz

Library of Congress Cataloging-in-Publication Data available.

ISBN 978-1-7972-1192-3

Manufactured in China.

Design by Rachel Harrell.

Post-it Brand is a trademark of 3M.

10 9 8 7 6 5 4 3 2 1

Chronicle books and gifts are available at special quantity discounts to corporations, professional associations, literacy programs, and other organizations. For details and discount information, please contact our premiums department at corporatesales@chroniclebooks.com or at 1-800-759-0190.

Chronicle Books LLC
680 Second Street
San Francisco, California 94107
www.chroniclebooks.com